HOW TO COMBAT
ANOREXIA, BULIMIA AND COMPULSIVE OVEREATING

HOW TO Combat

Anorexia Bulimia and Compulsive overeating

The Promis handbook on eating disorders and recovery.

Dr. Robert Lefever

Promis Publishing Limited
1 St. Quintin Avenue
London W10 6NX

First published 1988

ISBN 1 871013 04 6

Designed by Glenn Travis Associates, London

Printed in Great Britain by Biddles Limited, Guildford

To

Shirley Klein

in gratitude for her help
and encouragement

Contents

Acknowledgements

To Shirley Klein, Judi Hollis, Cindy Roschnotti, Gale Schneider, Fred Schneider and Steven Levenkron who first kindled my interest in eating disorders.

To my fellow board members of the International Association of Eating Disorder Professionals for their continuing stimulus.

To Beauchamp Colclough and all my colleagues, friends and patients in the PROMIS Recovery Centre and to many members of various Anonymous Fellowships who have taught me all I know about eating disorders, addiction and recovery.

To the staff and patients at the Hazelden Foundation in Minneapolis who first gave me formal and informal training.

To my partner, Guy Staight, and to our staff and patients at the PROMIS Unit in London.

To my wife and children for their understanding and for the happiness they give me.

To my secretary, Sarah Oaten, who patiently typed and re-typed this PROMIS Handbook.

To Alcoholics Anonymous World Services Inc for permission to reprint excerpts from "Alcoholics Anonymous", and "Twelve Steps and Twelve Traditions" and to Overeaters Anonymous for permission to reprint their Twelve Steps and Twelve Traditions. It should be emphasised that these excerpts are direct quotations from the literature of Alcoholics Anonymous and Overeaters Anonymous but that any opinions expressed in this PROMIS Handbook are those of its author.

Preface

Addictive disease is so widespread that it has some effect on the lives of almost all of us one way or another. Some people suffer from it, others have it in their families and many of us, as professionals or non-professionals, come across it in our work. Initially we believe that it could not happen to us or to our own family and that if it does turn up at work it will only be on rare occasions in rather strange or sad people who have experienced particular stress. But, as our knowledge and understanding increase, we see that addictive disease is mostly invisible simply because it is so very common. We do not see the hand in front of our face.

It can take many forms. Addiction can be to various substances, processes or relationships. Most common is alcoholism, although, as more becomes known about other forms of addictive disease, such as the eating disorders (compulsive overeating, bulimia and anorexia) we may find that they are just as widespread or perhaps they are simply the same disease in differing presentations. The illegal addictive drugs are increasingly commonly available and many legal (prescribed or over-the-counter) drugs may be little if any less addictive and damaging despite their legality. Gambling and various forms of risk-taking are far from simple pleasures in some people and workaholism may be far more than a semi-envious term of abuse. Some relationships can be addictive in their nature and just as destructive in their outcome as addiction to any substance or process.

It may be that addiction is part of the human condition: a potential in all of us. It seems more probable, however, that its potential is present only in some of us or at any rate that its potential in others is so weak as to be negligible.

But none of us can afford to ignore it. This handbook has been written not only to guide those whose professional work may lead them into direct contact with addictive disease in one or other of its forms but also to provide a basic understanding for anyone whose life may be affected by it directly or indirectly through someone else.

If you are concerned that you yourself or someone you know may have some form of inner compulsion that seems to be progressively destructive in its effects then this handbook is for you.

Contrary to common expectation, a general understanding of addictive disease and, in particular, a knowledge of the addictive nature of some drugs or other substances, including some normally classed as foods, is *not* in itself a disincentive to addiction. An addict will continue his or her addiction despite all the intellectual knowledge in the world: its relevance to him or her will simply be denied. That is the nature of addictive disease. This intellectual knowledge can be used, however, by others in order to identify those most at risk from developing the full-blown manifestations of addictive disease. It is therefore hoped that the information given in this handbook will give some insight into how individuals can best be protected from awakening an addictive potential.

Another common belief is that addiction is either untreatable or that it can only be "treated" by punitive measures of one kind or another (some of them administered by the medical profession) or by various forms of substitution or aversion therapy or by prolonged psychotherapy of one kind or another to discover "why" the individual became addicted. The belief of this handbook is that there is no "why" other than that some people just are like that. The psycho-social model of primary causation has no evidence to support it even though there are many psycho-social commonalities in the lives of sufferers from addictive disease during the active phase of their illness. Conversely, the recovery of a vast number of sufferers from addictive disease through various Anonymous Fellowships, such as Alcoholics Anonymous or Overeaters, Bulimics or Anorexics Anonymous, shows that anyone can recover regardless of psycho-social circumstances past or present. This handbook is therefore not simply a clinical treatise but more importantly a message of hope.

The PROMIS Handbook is intended to be read as a continuous narrative rather than as a subject reference book. To avoid repetition as far as possible, the concepts of one chapter or particular question and answer are carried over into succeeding chapters, questions and answers. For example, it is necessary to understand the concepts of the primary disease and of denial before reading about the family disease. Thus, the intention is to give a broad picture of addictive disease and to show how specific questions and answers fit into that broad picture and, more particularly, to show the commonality of all addictive disease and the common pathway to recovery.

1. The Disease Concept

Disease causes disturbance in function. Addictive disease causes the sufferer to return at some time to the substance, process or relationship of addiction despite various disturbances of function and despite previous negative consequences. Addiction is in the person, not just in the drug or substance or behaviour.

Consider Food:

It is a necessary ingredient in life for all of us.

It is part of each daily routine but also part of most celebrations. Mostly we take it for granted.

But some people do not appear to be able to use it responsibly. They appear to develop specific eating disorders that are addictive in nature, such as compulsive overeating, bulimia or anorexia.

How do you know if you are a compulsive over-eater?

The PROMIS Eating Disorder Questionnaires assesses whether you have a compulsive or addictive relationship with food or whether you are simply greedy on occasions:

(a) *Bingeing*

1. Does your mouth *almost invariably* pour with water when you look at a menu before a meal or when you look at illustrations of dishes you know you would like?
2. Do you get irritable and impatient at meal times when there is a gap of ten minutes between courses?
3. Would it be more painful for you to give up sugar and white flour - and therefore everything that contains sugar and white flour - than to give up a close friendship.
4. Do you not infrequently have your mouth so full with one fork or spoonful after another that it is difficult or almost impossible to chew?

5. Do you tend to swallow food after chewing it only once or twice?
6. Do you almost prefer to eat alone rather than in company?
7. Have you *often* eaten more than just a bite or two last thing at night or taken food to bed with you?
8. Do you *particularly* enjoy eating *all* the dried out crusts on a plate or dish or saucepan?
9. Do you tend to think of food not so much as a satisfier of hunger but as a reward that you deserve because of stress you endure?
10. Have you ever eaten a whole bowl of burnt porridge or something similarly considered to be inedible?
11. Do you feel in a strange way that you have an intimate relationship with food and that you become a "real" person when you are involved in your particular way with food?
12. Do you finish off, straight from the refrigerator, the cold leftovers from a meal several days previously or soft cheeses that have gone hard and crusted?
13. Do you prefer to "graze" like a cow throughout the day rather than ever allow yourself to get hungry?
14. Do you tend to use food as *both* a comfort and strength even when you are not at all hungry?
15. When you have *definitely* eaten too much do you tend to feel defiant as well as disappointed in yourself?
16. When you are eating in company do you tend to time your eating as a form of strategy so that others are not really aware of precisely how little or how much you are eating?
17. Would you almost rather eat bread and jam at the time you expected to have a meal rather than wait half an hour for Cordon Bleu.?
18. Have you ever regularly stolen or helped yourself to other peoples' sweets or food even though you had enough money to buy your own?
19. Do you find it difficult to leave anything on your plate?
20. Do you find that being full is often irrelevant in deciding when to stop eating?
21. Do you find that you sometimes put on weight even when you are trying to diet?
22. Are you aware from your own experience that some substances act as "trigger" foods so that, once started, it is difficult to control further eating?

23. Are you afraid that you will put an *excessive* amount of weight on if you give up smoking or using laxatives or appetite suppressants or self-induced vomiting or exercising or give up strict control of food intake?

24. Do you actively prefer restaurants where they serve large portions, even when you are not concerned with the cost?

25. Have you ever had three or more different sizes of clothes in your adult, non-pregnant, wardrobe?

26. Has anyone else expressed repeated serious concern over your eating habits, body weight or shape?

27. Would you eat a full meal in response to an unexpected invitation despite having already eaten a full meal?

28. Would you think it wasteful if any of the dishes in an Indian or Chinese meal are left unfinished and would you therefore finish them even if you are not hungry *and* are other people's leftovers generally fair game for you to finish off?

29. Do you find that *all* of these questions are perfectly straightforward and *none* of them a bit strange?

30. Do you feel that you would instinctively understand someone who answered yes to *all* of these questions?

(b) *Starving*

1. In a restaurant or even at home do you not infrequently try to persuade other people to choose dishes that you know you would like even though you yourself would probably refuse to eat them?

2. Do you get irritable and impatient at mealtimes if someone tries to persuade you to eat something?

3. Would it be more painful for you to give up sugar and white flour – and therefore everything that contains sugar and white flour – than to give up a close friendship?

4. Do you not infrequently chew something and then take it out of your mouth and throw it away?

5. When you swallow food does it often tend to make you feel unhappy, queasy, and bloated?

6. On the occasions that you eat at all, do you prefer to eat alone rather than in company?

7. Have you often tried to empty your body of as much fluid as possible so that you feel at peace before going to bed at night?

8. Do you *particularly* enjoy eating raw vegetables and also salty or sour things?

9. Do you tend to think of losing weight and changing your body shape as a reward that you deserve because of stress you endure?

10. Have you ever had a list of so many things that you dare not eat, that there is very little left that you can eat?

11. Do you feel in a strange way that you are "understoood" by food and that you have a particular intimate relationship with it and that you only become a "real" person when eating particular foods or abstaining altogether from eating?

12. Does the smell of some food make you wish that you could eat it like other people do but do you nonetheless find that you cannot bring yourself to do so?

13. Do you not uncommonly find that you are no longer hungry even if you have not eaten for a day or two or even more?

14. Do you tend to reduce your intake of liquids in order to give yourself a feeling of comfort and strength?

15. When you do eat something reasonably substantial do you tend to feel disappointed or even angry with yourself as well as slightly relieved?

16. When you are eating in company do you tend to time your eating as a form of strategy so that others are not really aware of precisely how little you are eating?

17. Have you often simply absented yourself at mealtimes or said, substantially untruthfully, that you have already eaten?

18. Have you ever regularly stolen or helped yourself to other people's sweets or food even though you had enough money to buy your own?

19. Do you find it difficult to finish everything on your plate, almost regardless of how little you put on it in the first place?

20. Do you hate feeling full and find it virtually impossible to eat any more when you have that feeling?

21. Do you find that you sometimes lose weight even though you were not specifically intending to do so?

22. Are you aware from your own experience that some substances act as "trigger" foods so that, once started, it is difficult to control further eating?

23. Are you afraid that you will put on an *excessive* amount of weight if you give up smoking or using laxatives or appetite supressants or

self-induced vomiting or exercising or give up strict control of food intake?

24. If you go out in company to a restaurant do you prefer simply to drink some tea or coffee or have a diet drink while everyone else is eating?

25. Have you ever had three or more different sizes of clothes in your adult, non-pregnant wardrobe.

26. Has anyone else expressed repeated, serious, concern over your eating habits, body weight or shape?

27. If you find that you have put on some weight do you commonly stop eating altogether for a day or two?

28. If you do eat in company do you like to be with special friends or family members whom you can rely upon to finish off some foods for you?

29. Do you find that all of these questions are perfectly straightforward and none of them a bit strange?

30. Do you feel you would instinctively understand someone who answered yes to *all* of these questions?

A full analysis of the answers to these questions will be delayed while three further questions are asked.

How do you know if you are bulimic?

Bulimia means "to have a voracious appetite" or to eat like an animal, gulping the food down as if in fear that the supply will run out.

Bulimia does *not* mean self-induced vomiting. Most commonly people who force vomit *are* bulimic but they are not necessarily so, just as all people who have a consistently high alcohol consumption are not necessarily alcoholic, although most commonly they are.

Bulimia therefore refers to the way someone eats rather than to the methods he or she uses to avoid the consequence of getting fat from overeating. Thus, bulimia is the same as compulsive overeating and can be assessed using the same questionnaire.

Customarily the term bulimia refers to repeated self-induced vomiting. This is incorrect because the term is more helpfully restricted to those who have compulsive or addictive disease and are distressed to find that they cannot help themselves. Others may simply be following a "craze" or habit of self-induced vomiting, as is not uncommon in schoolgirls, particularly when under acute stress such as when there are impending examinations. Some others may be protecting themselves from occasional lapses of greed while trying to follow the contemporary cultural dictates of fashion. Nonetheless, if someone does force vomit *at all* it is advisable to give serious consideration to this being due to compulsive or addictive disease because it is only too easy to rationalise it away as something that is simply a craze or habit.

In this respect it is both interesting and alarming to note that in recent years fashion has decreed that women become progressively thinner and that both men and women become progressively more physically fit. Physical fitness is admirable in itself but can be used compulsively or addictively as a means of using up excess calories and to maintain or strive to achieve a body image that may in truth be inappropriate. It is often thought that the "image makers" in the media are therefore responsible for people becoming anorexic or bulimic. This is not true. The still or television camera in close up makes people look fatter than they actually are because light rays converge towards the lens. Therefore, fashion models need to be thin in order to look "normal". However, this also means that "normal" shaped people look fatter in close up photographs than they actually are.

The problems of addictive disease go in parallel with a distortion of body image so that the sufferer has a different perception of his or her true shape from that which other people perceive him or her to be. In each case the sufferer tends to perceive himself or herself to be nearer to the norm than other people would say. Thus, someone who is excessively fat and someone who is excessively thin from compulsive or addictive disease both may have an image of themselves that is nearer to the norm than is appropriate. This is due to the distortions of perception that are part of compulsive or addictive disease itself and nothing to do with the distortions of the camera lens or the dictates of fashion.

Nonetheless, people who habitually force vomit do form a particular sub-group of compulsive over eaters. But the crucial realisation is that their compulsion or addiction is *not* cured simply by desisting from vomiting: they may simply be moving into a different phase of the over all pattern of eating disorders. Thus, the PROMIS Eating Disorders Questionnaire has been designed to look for compulsive or addictive disease in *any* phase. Someone who is no longer vomiting may therefore still be bulimic in the true sense of the term and the PROMIS Eating Disorders Questionnaire will assess that.

How do you know if you are anorexic?

Anorexia means "loss of appetite". This can happen in many physical or emotional conditions. Anorexia nervosa, however, is a specific clinical condition in which the sufferer progressively starves himself or herself, saying that he or she is not hungry and that he or she eats quite sufficient for his or her needs, despite all objective evidence to the contrary.

As already explained in the section on bulimia, the body image of any sufferer from an eating disorder may be far removed from reality. Thus, the sufferer from anorexia nervosa may be emaciated and yet still be convinced that he or she is "normal" or even "fat". It is therefore exceedingly difficult to convince a sufferer from anorexia nervosa that he or she is actually underweight, whatever the scales may say. The accuracy of the scales or of the charts that list the normal weights for various heights and builds and the accuracy of *other* peoples' observations and perceptions may all be hotly disputed.

Anorexia nervosa is *not* "the slimmers disease" as it is often described. Sufferers do not become anorexic by going too far in a normal slimming routine. At any one time vast numbers of people are on diets in order to lose weight. Few of them will have eating disorders as such. Most will be struggling to fit into clothes that they believe make them more attractive or struggling to take off a few pounds that resulted from a period of self-indulgence or merely from the passing of the years. However, it is important to be aware that these are exactly the rationalisations that sufferers from eating disorders give to their own attempts to change their body weight or shape.

The French have obligingly discovered a mysterious fluid called "cellulite" that comes from nowhere and causes women to bulge in all the "wrong" places. Cellulite is in fact normal fat (which is indeed fluid at normal body temperature) and its deposition throughout the body is determined by normal female hormones.

Fat comes from food and should not be confused with fluid retention which can be caused by variations in hormone secretion (fluid retention increases pre-menstrually) or by other medical conditions such as thyroid deficiency. Again, hormonal imbalance or thyroid deficiency are common rationalisations used by sufferers from eating disorders and others to give pseudo-scientific explanations to what may, more truthfully, be the product either of compulsive or addictive disease or, alternatively,of mere self-indulgence. Only relatively rarely is there genuine hormonal imbalance, thyroid deficiency or other clinical conditions causing fluid retention. These conditions are generally clinically correctable and therefore no cause for continuing disorder of food intake or body weight or shape.

It should be noted, however, that the body soon becomes accustomed to the regular intake of fluid-reducing tablets (diuretics) or thyroid hormones or appetite supressants or laxatives. Discontinuing any of these substances after regular use therefore has a rebound effect in which the individual does indeed swell up. This may erroneously be taken as proof of the body's need for the medicines. In truth it means nothing of the kind: the body has become habituated to those substances and needs time to re-establish its own self-regulatory mechanisms.

Some foods – salty substances, raw vegetables, health foods and other specific foods – appeal particularly to sufferers from Anorexia. They may persuade themselves that they are eating large quantities of food even though the low calorie count ensures continued weight stability or loss.

In all the eating disorders the process of bingeing or starving results in an emotional "high" and is used as a method of suppressing other emotional feelings.

Anorexia and Bulimia are not clearly distinct conditions. The same individual may sufferer from both conditions at different times or have some features of both conditions at the same time. Thus, someone who is primarily in an anorexic phase, using starvation as his or her prime method of control over emotions and relationships, may have episodes of bingeing and then starve again as a method of gaining further, illusory, control and in order to control the physical consequences of the binge. Similarly, someone who is primarily in a bulimic phase of the disease may binge on lettuce or on other foodstuffs that have particularly low calorie value and weight-producing potential or may even control body weight by dramatically reducing fluid intake. Therefore they may actually lose weight even though apparently consuming large quantities of food.

At both extremes of anorexia or bulimia the sufferers may use medications to induce vomiting or to reduce body fluid or to purge themselves either with laxatives or enemas or both.

The relationships between eating disorders and compulsive physical exercise may be totally intertwined. Physical exercise also has the capacity to be used to attempt to control emotional feelings, to work off the calories consumed in food and to control body size. Thus the compulsive relationship with physical exercise can become effectively part of the spectrum of eating disorder behaviour.

There is evidence that some people, relative to others, are "underburners" in their body metabolism so that they become more efficient biochemical users of food. The same intake of food as other people results in a relative excess above their needs and therefore an increase in fat storage. The variations in basic body biochemistry between one human being and another may be of some clinical significance in this respect and may indicate a genetic predisposition to obesity, although not necessarily to compulsive overeating.

"Over or under-burning" may at times be no more than a further rationalisation used by some sufferers from eating disorders to give an "explanation" for their condition.

Thus, the rationalisations of sufferers from eating disorders are many and various and may be hotly defended. But so are the rationalisations of those who are merely self indulgent. Those who watch with incredibility as sufferers from anorexia starve themselves towards death in their particular delusion may do well to examine the intensity with which they defend their own concepts on cellulite, hormonal imbalance, thyroid deficiency, underburning and the rest.

Anorexia nervosa is the same compulsive or addictive disease as compulsive overeating or bulimia. The sufferer from anorexia clings to self control even to the extent of risking and sometimes losing life itself. It is often thought that people who suffer from compulsive or addictive disorders, such as alcoholism or drug addiction or the eating disorders, do so primarily as a result of loss of self control, with psychological and social factors as the underlying causes. Observing sufferers from anorexia shows how far this viewpoint is from the truth: there is no greater self control than is seen in the sufferer from anorexia determinedly refusing life-sustaining food.

The reason that the food is refused is because it is not perceived as life-sustaining at all. Quite the opposite: it is seen as life-threatening. The sufferer fears that once the control is relaxed then there is no knowing when a subsequent binge will stop. Many compulsive overeaters demonstrate this point by referring to an earlier time in their lives when they were anorexic. At the same time a sufferer from anorexia becomes addicted to the physical, emotional and mental aspects of starvation itself.

Thus, anorexia nervosa is a defense mechanism against the fears of compulsive overeating just as self-induced vomiting can be a form of protection against the obese consequences of compulsive overeating. There is therefore just one primary addictive disease – compulsive overeating – even though it may seem bizarre to refer to someone wasting away from anorexia nervosa as being fundamentally a compulsive overeater. But this is the case.

Thus, the *bingeing* PROMIS Eating Disorders Questionnaire has been designed also to reveal anorexia nervosa because it reveals compulsive or addictive disease in *any* phase. For someone in an anorexic phase the questions should be preceded by the phrase "if you *were* to eat . . ." or "If you *were* to give up control . . ." or "When you *were* eating . . ." Correspondingly, in the case of compulsive overeating or Bulimia, the questions in the *starving* Questionnaire may be preceded by the phrase "if you were to starve yourself . . .'

What is bulimarexia?

A long word invented by doctors who do not understand the interrelationship between compulsive overeating, bulimia and anorexia nervosa. It simply gives an unnecessary name to the state where sufferers from the compulsive or addictive disease of compulsive overeating try to control their binges either through bingeing on non-fattening foods such as lettuce or by drinking vast quantities of water or by excessive use of purgatives or by avoiding food altogether for a time.

Giving individual names to different phases of what is basically one and the same condition is counterproductive. The sufferers may come to believe that they are special and different from sufferers from other forms of eating disorders and different altogether from sufferers from other forms of compulsive or addictive disease. Neither is the case.

How does one interpret the answers to the PROMIS Eating Disorders Questionnaires?

A positive answer to *ANY* question may just possibly be an indication of a compulsive or addictive disorder of some kind.

This may seem excessively severe and even extreme but the questions are specifically designed to look for compulsive or addictive characteristics. Someone who has no form of addictive disease will most commonly answer "no" to all the questions. Conversely, however, there may be false positive answers from some people who may be overanxious by nature or who may find questionnaires confusing or imprecise.

The difficulty is that the primary psycho-pathology of any addictive disease is "denial". The prime psychological feature of addictive disease is that it tells you that you do not have it. The sufferers from alcoholism often believe that they may have problems with stress or depression but no real problem with alcohol and they may sometimes be supported in this view by their families and even by their doctors. So also the sufferers from drug addiction may have given up drugs many times, thereby spuriously "proving" to themselves that they are not addicted – but never wondering how it is that they are nonetheless repeatedly drawn back to one mood-altering substance or another. Similarly, the sufferers from eating disorders may accept that they have problems with body weight or shape but adamantly refuse to consider that their relationship with food may be basically compulsive or addictive in nature.

Thus, in questionnaires designed by people who think in terms of drunkeness and of "safe" units of alcohol consumed and of "sensible drinking programmes'' the sufferer from alcoholism may happily tick off all the ''no'' answers. Not only do those questionnaires tend to lack insight into the nature of addictive disease but also there may be little awareness of the sheer intensity of denial that can result in the sufferer from alcoholism simply not making any mental connection between the alcohol consumed and the various damaging events that are in fact direct consequences.

Similarly, sufferers from eating disorders may blithely tick off all the ''no'' answers even in the PROMIS Eating Disorder Questionnaires or more commonly in questionnaires designed by people who are not aware that the Eating Disorders form part of the spectrum of addictive disease.

Despite denial, the sufferer often has an inner fear of insanity or uncontrolability in the awareness that food is beginning to control many aspects of life and not simply satisfy the need for biochemical fuel. Coupled to this is the desperate fear that there appears to be no way out: all diets and other methods of external control have failed. Furthermore, the strength of the addictive relationship with particular substances or patterns of behaviour may be so great as to make the prospect of doing without them unthinkable. As a result of a combination of these various factors, the sufferer may put down a whole row of ''no'' answers even when knowing inwardly that some or even almost all of the answers should have been ''yes''. Consequently, if even one positive answer slips through the defensive net it may be an indication that there is need for further assessment by counselling staff specialising in addictive disease.

As with assessment for other forms of addictive disease, it may be most helpful to go through the PROMIS Eating Disorders Questionnaires with someone else. Many of the questions are subjective, answerable only by the sufferer, but some have objective features and could be answered by anyone who knows the sufferer well. However, sometimes that other person may be too close to be able to see clearly and may have intense emotional commitment to concepts and potential solutions of his or her own and therefore be unable to give a truly objective assessment. Best of all is to go through the questionnaire with a counsellor specialising in eating disorders.

The general rule-of-thumb interpretation of the PROMIS Eating Disorder Questionnaire is as follows:

i. Zero positive answers indicates no addictive disease.

ii. One to five positive answers indicates the possibility of addictive disease of some kind but probably no significant cross-addiction with food.

iii. Six to nine positive answers indicates a greater possibility of addictive disease of some kind and quite possibly an eating disorder. Further assessment will be necessary.

iv. Ten to nineteen positive answers indicates addictive disease of some kind and also a definite cross-addiction with food. Those sufferers will need to deal with their eating disorder as well as deal with what they considered to be their primary addiction involving their drug or behaviour of choice. Failure to deal with their eating disorder will result in recovery being stunted so that there is a high risk of relapse.

v. Twenty or more positive answers indicates addictive disease with food as the primary drug of choice. These sufferers may or may not have other cross addictions.

What is the significance of each individual question in the PROMIS Eating Disorders Questionnaire?

(a) *Bingeing*

1. Does your mouth *almost invariably* pour with water when you look at a menu before a meal or when you look at illustrations of dishes you know you would like?

Question 1 looks for the specific "drug of choice" that is a specific feature for each sufferer from addictive disease. This physiological response to food for the sufferer from an eating disorder is the equivalent of the anticipatory excitement for sufferers from any other form of addictive disease when contemplating use of their own specific "drug of choice".

2. Do you get irritable and impatient at meal times when there is a gap of ten minutes between courses?

Question 2. The "theme song" of any addictive disease is "I want what I want when I want it and I want it *now*." A wait of half an hour between courses would try anybody"s patience but ten minutes is socially acceptable to all but the sufferers from eating disorders. Once started on any particular meal they like to continue uninterrupted. Even conversation may be an irritant. They would tend to ensure that there is still a supply of bread or something similar to tide over the gap.

3. Would it be more painful for you to give up sugar and white flour – and therefore everything that contains sugar and white flour than to give up a close friendship?

Question 3 looks at the intensity of the relationship with the eating disorder sufferers' primary drugs of choice: sugar and white flour. These are the exact equivalent of alcohol for the sufferer from alcoholism or of cocaine, cannabis, heroin, amphetamines, solvents, Valium or some other specific mood-altering drug of choice for sufferers from drug addiction. Similarly, it is the equivalent of the crucial first card or spin or "go" for the compulsive gambler, the first cigarette for the nicotine addict, the first cup of tea, coffee, chocolate or glass of coca cola or lemonade for the caffeine addict and so on. The intensity of the relationship is something only another addict can understand. Frequently, well-meaning friends or helpers may say "Well, I gave up smoking (or whatever) . . ." without any insight into the fact that for them smoking (or whatever) was simply a habit and not the truly addictive process that some other smokers (or other users) find when they simply *cannot* give up however hard they try. Indeed, even the sufferers themselves may be unaware of the extreme difficulty of giving up sugar and white flour until they try to do so.

Given the severe choice of "drugs" or home, an addict will commonly choose drugs. The relationship between an addict of any kind and his or her drug of choice is the primary relationship of life. It is clung to until almost, or even absolutely, everything else is destroyed. The relationship is stronger than many human relationships and is so special (in a way that other people find strange and upsetting) that an addict may say that he or she only feels "understood" by his or her drug. *This* is the intensity of addiction: the feeling that human relationships may come and go but the relationship with the drug of choice is intensely personal and private, special and different. Interestingly, the addictive relationship with sugar and white flour (and with anything containing these substances) is often not recognised until an attempt is made to give them up. Withdrawal symptoms of headaches, dizziness and irritability may then be very severe.

4. Do you not infrequently have your mouth so full with one fork or spoonful after another that it is difficult or almost impossible to chew?

Question 4 illustrates the impossibility of satisfying a craving. Compulsive overeaters do not eat because they are hungry but because they crave. As with alcohol for the sufferer from alcoholism, the first "dose" of sugar or white flour in any day may or may not trigger a binge. This can be very confusing for all manner of addicts: the first use does *not* always trigger an uncontrolled response. But it *may* do so and in time, in recovery from addiction, the recovering person learns not to risk the first compulsive use in any day. For sufferers from eating disorders, sugar and white flour are the principal "drugs" but other substances may have similar "trigger" effects in some people. Thus all wheat products, dairy products and all manner of foods, single or multiple, *may* act as "triggers".

Some people who give up sugar and white flour altogether may find that they still overeat and that other substances take the place of sugar as "trigger" foods. But it is fallacious to believe that a person in recovery from an eating disorder will have a particularly difficult challenge in comparison to people recovering from other addictions because he or she has to negotiate a relationship with his or her drug of choice at three mealtimes every day. This is untrue and is simply yet another rationalisation. The person in recovery from an eating disorder has first only to put down sugar and white flour and foods that contain them and also avoid other food substances that cause particular craving. This is the exact parallel to the person in recovery from alcoholism first having to put down alcohol and all other mood-altering substances that are known to be cross-addictive with alcohol. But the sufferer from alcoholism can still drink milk or orange juice or many other things: it is only alcohol that must be avoided. Similarly, sufferers from eating disorders need only avoid these specific foods.

In the eating disorders, alcoholism and other addictions, there is a great deal more to recovery than this first step of physical abstinence but this first step is essential as is the realisation that there is nothing special and different about eating disorders. Both the disease and the recovery process follow the same pattern for all addictions and recovery.

The crucial initial issue, however, for the sufferers from an eating disorder is not to find out which foods are fattening (that is the function of diet regimes and these have no effect on addiction) but rather to become aware of which foods may set off a craving. Once this craving is stimulated, the sufferer from an eating disorder will eat anything.

5. Do you tend to swallow food after chewing it only once of twice?

Question 5 shows that eating fast is not in itself evidence of compulsive overeating. Some people just do normally eat faster than others. But the compulsive overeater is trying to fill an inner sense of emptiness that in fact is emotional rather than physical in origin. But high food intake results in serotonin secretion in the brain and serotonin is one of the body's natural tranquillisers. Thus, the inner void *is* satisfied by compulsive overeating just as alcohol or drugs *do* alter the mood. Gulping food down is therefore using food for its tranquillising effect rather than using it for its taste or nutritional value.

6. Do you almost prefer to eat alone rather than in company?

Question 6 again illustrates the primary nature of the relationship between an addict and his or her drug of choice. Conversation and even basic table manners and civilities get in the way.

7. Have you *often* eaten more than just a bite or two last thing at night or taken food to bed with you?

Question 7 particularly shows the level of pre-occupation with food that is part of compulsive overeating. It is not simply that the sufferer is being cautious in planning ahead, it is more that he or she fears or may even *hope* to wake up in the middle of the night but at least will have a further dose of "tranquilliser" readily available.

8. Do you *particularly* enjoy eating *all* the dried out crusts on a plate or dish or saucepan?

Question 8 demonstrates that compulsive overeaters know exactly where the strongest flavours are to be found and would not dream of wasting any of them. Strong flavours tend to give strong emotional rewards but may stimulate further appetite.

9. Do you tend to think of food not so much as a satisfier of hunger but as a reward that you deserve because of stress you endure?

Question 9 particularly illustrates the medicinal, tranquillising, effect of food so that it is used in response to stress rather than hunger. Many people "reward" themselves with an occasional meal or drink without this implying that they are suffering from an eating disorder or from alcoholism. But they would normally eat and drink in response to hunger and thirst and would develop other forms of response to stress – such as tackling the source of specific stresses. For the addict there is no great advantage in resolving particular stresses – that would close down a principal rationalisation for continuing to use the substance or behaviour of addiction. For the addict the substance or behaviour of addiction is *always* a reward and therefore it becomes the favoured reward, regardless of its relevance to other circumstances such as hunger or thirst or emotional pain.

10. Have you ever eaten a whole bowl of burnt porridge or something similarly considered to be inedible?

Question 10 looks again at the compulsive overeater's use of the tranquillising effect of food – regardless of its taste.

11. Do you feel in a strange way that you have an intimate relationship with food and that you become a "real" person when you are involved in your particular way with food?

Question 11 illustrates the crude intimacy of the relationship between the compulsive overeater and his or her drug and gives a further reason for preferring to eat alone. The compulsive overeater will attack food in the same way that a cat will snatch at its food, even if it comes from a tin and cannot run away. In recovery the compulsive overeater will discover the need to have three set meals daily and not allow his or her teeth to get into anything else at any other time.

Again it is not primarily a question of the calories that may be consumed but rather that the first compulsive bite may be rationalised into a need for "a little something" and on further into a full scale binge on the grounds that, once daily abstinence is blown, he or she might just as well go the whole hog for the rest of the day and then start abstinence all over again the following day.

12. Do you finish off, straight from the refrigerator, the cold leftovers from a meal several days previously or soft cheeses that have gone hard and crusted?

Question 12 again emphasises that taste, temperature and appearance are not as significant as timing. *Now* is what counts.

13. Do you prefer to "graze" like a cow throughout the day rather than ever allow yourself to get hungry?

Question 13 yet again illustrates the tranquillising effect of food. Maintenance doses may only be small but they keep the tranquillising effect "topped-up". The social purpose of meals may be totally ignored. Hunger may not be allowed at all for fear that the response cannot be controlled. However, the sufferer may delude himself or herself by thinking that only small quantities are consumed by grazing: simply vast amounts may be shovelled away as from a conveyor belt.

14. Do you tend to use food as *both* a comfort and strength even when you are not at all hungry?

Question 14 particularly illustrates that the compulsive overeater eats for emotional rather than physical reasons.

15. When you have *definitely* eaten too much do you tend to feel defiant as well as disappointed in yourself?

Question 15 is particularly important because it demonstrates the difference between the addictive disease and the suffering individual that it inflicts. The individual is pathetically disappointed whereas the disease, as an alien parasite affecting mind and behaviour, is defiant. The capacity to see this differentiation between the suffering individual and the afflicting addictive disease is crucial to the disease concept of addiction. Traditionally, addiction tends to be thought of as the product of weak will and of disturbance in psychological and social background. The disease concept, adopted in Minnesota Method treatment centres, based upon the principles of Alcoholics Anonymous and other Anonymous Fellowships, holds that background is not a primary determinant and that strong rather than weak will is a cause of problems and, further, that addictive disease affects some people but not others and that it is not the fault of the sufferer, nor within his or her control.

16. When you are eating in company do you tend to time your eating as a form of strategy so that others are not really aware of precisely how little or how much you are eating?

Question 16 is another crucially important question because it demonstrates the sufferer's self obsession and the consequent need to be aware of what everyone else around him or her is doing in relation to food. The food is the primary relationship that rivets his or her attention, not the people. The perceived need to disguise from others (commonly unsuccessfully) the exact amount of food consumed is part of the delusion of addictive disease. In the first place other people are not particularly interested and secondly they are not fooled anyway. Again, the parallel is with the sufferer from alcoholism who believes that he or she is disguising the total consumption from others whereas in truth the only person deceived is himself or herself.

17. Would you almost rather eat bread and jam at the time you expected to have a meal rather than wait half an hour for Cordon Bleu?

Question 17 illustrates the compulsive overeater's obsession with predictable regularity of supply of food. The unpredictable is very unsettling and therefore precautions may be taken.

18. Have you ever regularly stolen or helped yourself to other people's sweets or food even though you had enough money to buy your own?

Question 18 shows the disease protecting its supply routes. In parallel with other forms of addictive disease, it also shows the distressing disparity between values and behaviour that may open up in the life of the compulsive overeater. Initially, there are determined efforts to force the behaviour to comply with the values. However, as the addictive disease progressively worsens and behaviour gets worse along with it, the gap between values and behaviour becomes unbridgeable. At this point there is a serious risk of suicide. Significant numbers of sufferers from addictive disease opt for that tragic way out because they have no concept of alternative solutions. Alternatively, they adjust their values to comply with their behaviour and the trail of progressive degradation continues.

19. Do you find it difficult to leave anything on your plate?

Question 19 shows again that hunger is not relevant to the amount consumed and also illustrates the fear of getting hungry before the next meal.

20. Do you find that being full is often irrelevant in deciding when to stop eating?

Question 20 is the same as question 19 expressed in more explicit form.

21. Do you find that you sometimes put on weight even when you are trying to diet?

Question 21 illustrates the impossibility of dietary solutions to the compulsions of addictive disease.

22. Are you aware from your own experience that some substances act as a "trigger" foods so that, once started, it is difficult to control further eating?

Question 22 is asking the specific question about trigger foods. Many sufferers from eating disorders would answer "no" to this question not only because it never occured to them to look but also because the disease does not want them to look and therefore, in subconscious denial, they simply do not see. Again, it may seem positively wierd to refer to the disease as if it had an entity of its own, with its own mind and behaviour, - but addictive disease does indeed behave exactly like that.

23. Are you afraid that you will put on *excessive* amounts of weight if you give up smoking or using laxatives or appetite suppressants or self-induced vomiting or exercising or give up strict control of food intake?

Question 23 is the crucial question for any sufferer from addictive disease and particularly for sufferers in the anorexic or bulimic phases of the addictive eating disorders. (Now using bulimic in its coloquial meaning of compulsive enforced vomiting and in the sense that it will be used for the rest of this Handbook). Any of the processes referred to can be simply methods of trying to pre-empt - or to control the consequences of - compulsive overeating.

24. Do you actively prefer restaurants where they serve large portions, even when you are not concerned with the cost?

Question 24 looks again at the adjustment of values to comply with behaviour and also looks at the generally higher capacity for food that, through constant training, compulsive overeaters will have acquired relative to the general population.

25. Have you ever had three or more different sizes of clothes in your adult, non-pregnant, wardrobe?

Question 25 looks pragmatically at the failure of dietary solutions. The weight may come off but it goes back on again.

26. Has anyone else expressed repeated serious concern over your eating habits, body weight or shape?

Question 26 attempts to obtain some objectivity but the disease may quickly rationalise it away by making out in the sufferer's mind that the *other* person has problems of perception.

27. Would you eat a full meal in response to an unexpected invitation despite having already eaten a full meal?

Question 27 looks at the higher capacity than others, at the irrelevance of hunger, at the triggering effect and at the protection of supply. It is such an obvious question that it risks getting a flat denial even when the sufferer remembers specific occasions only too well. The shame of admitting it may be just too great. On the other hand, when the suffering is so great as to cause desperation, this question may tip the balance into giving up the struggle of denial.

28. Would you think it wasteful if any of the dishes in an Indian or Chinese meal are left unfinished and would you therefore finish them even if you are not hungry *and* are other people's leftovers generally fair game for you to finish off?

Question 28 again looks at increased capacity for food and at triggering and at protection of supply but here looks specifically at "waste", which is something that concerns many "normal" people but which is also a common rationalisation in compulsive overeating.

29. Do you find that *all* of these questions are perfectly straightforward and *none* of them a bit strange?

Question 29 is an attempt to force the sufferer to come down on one side or the other. The dilemma is that if he or she says that some of the questions are strange (as the disease would wish and as other people would genuinely say) then that would be the ultimate self-denial and giving in to the disease. As the sufferer progress through the questions, he or she will secretly have realised that they are the "right" questions: that they could only have been asked by people who have had first hand experience of an addictive eating disorder. Thus, there is a stark choice: go with the questioner or go with the disease. Superficially it may appear that someone with a kindly disposition or detached clinical interest might answer "yes" to this question and therefore the sufferer might answer "yes" in the hope of telling the truth – but at the same time not *really* being disloyal to the disease, the primary subject of relationship in life. But the trap for the disease is sprung: nobody but another sufferer would think that *all* the questions were straightforward and *none* of them strange.

30. Do you feel you would instinctively understand someone who answered yes to *all* of these questions?

Question 30 tries to cement the relationship with the questioner. The loneliness of the inner awareness – that other people find some or even all of the sufferer's behaviour towards food to be strange or bizarre or weird – can at last begin to be dispelled by sharing it with one other human being. Having demonstrated that *one* other person (the questioner) has shared the same thoughts and fears, humiliations and degradations and yet somehow has survived, then the sufferer may come to believe that perhaps there is hope after all.

(b) *Starving*

1. In a restaurant or even at home do you not infrequently try to persuade other people to choose dishes that you know you would like even though you yourself would probably refuse to eat them?

Question 1 looks at the addictive "behaviour of choice" of starving. Other people may be encouraged to eat but the sufferer chooses to starve.

2. Do you get irritable and impatient at mealtimes if someone tries to persuade you to eat something?

Question 2 looks at the preoccupation with being "perfectly normal" and the resentment felt for anyone not accepting that.

3. Would it be more painful for you to give up sugar and white flour – and therefore everything that contains sugar and white flour – than to give up a close friendship?

Question 3 is the same as for bingeing. Sufferers from anorexia will commonly say that they eat little sugar or white flour in any case. This is true but nonetheless they may crave them, and have cravings "triggered" by them, just the same as any other sufferer from an Eating Disorder.

4. Do you not infrequently chew something and then take it out of your mouth and throw it away?

Question 4 shows that once committed to starving in any day the sufferer from anorexia finds the prospect of swallowing exceedingly disturbing and threatening and may therefore repeatedly avoid it.

5. When you swallow food does it often tend to make you feel unhappy, queasy, and bloated?

Question 5 emphasises in greater detail the point already made in question 4.

6. On the occasions that you eat at all, do you prefer to eat alone rather than in company?

Question 6 emphasises the primary importance of the relationship with food or starvation as of more importance than other human contact.

7. Have you often tried to empty your body of as much fluid as possible so that you feel at peace before going to bed at night?

Question 7 shows the preoccupation with internal feeling to such an extent that it would prevent sleep if not appeased.

8. Do you *particularly* enjoy eating raw vegetables and also salty or sour things?

Question 8 shows that some vegetables are referred to specifically as "anorectic" vegetables because of their negligible calorific value. Salt kills all other flavour when taken in excess and hence turns off further appetite.

9. Do you tend to think of losing weight and changing your body shape as a reward that you deserve because of stress you endure?

Question 9 looks for the mood-altering properties as the true rewards of changes in body weight or shape. This is to some extent normal in both sexes – but not normal in the extent to which the process is taken in anorexia.

10. Have you ever had a list of so many things that you dare not eat, that there is very little left that you can eat?

Question 10 shows that the tranquillising effect of starvation gradually dominates everything else.

11. Do you feel in a strange way that you are "understoood" by food and that you have a particular intimate relationship with it and that you only become a "real" person when eating particular foods or abstaining altogether from eating?

Question 11 demonstrates the intimacy of the relationship between the sufferer and the addictive process.

12. Does the smell of some food make you wish that you could eat it like other people do but do you nonetheless find that you cannot bring yourself to do so?

Question 12 illustrates that the preference for eating alone is partly to avoid the natural physiological responses being stimulated by someone else's eating.

13. Do you not uncommonly find that you are no longer hungry even if you have not eaten for a day or two or even more?

Question 13 shows the addictive capacity to over-ride the standard physiological response of hunger: the urge to starve is stronger than the urge to eat.

14. Do you tend to reduce your intake of liquids in order to give yourself a feeling of comfort and strength?

Question 14 emphasises the emotional rather than purely physical effects of starving.

15. When you do eat something reasonably substantial do you tend to feel disappointed or even angry with yourself as well as slightly relieved?

Question 15, as in the *bingeing* questionnaire, demonstrates the difference between the disease and the suffering individual.

16. When you are eating in company do you tend to time your eating as a form of strategy so that others are not really aware of precisely how little you are eating?

Question 16 is the same as for the *bingeing* questionnaire.

17. Have you often simply absented yourself at mealtimes or said, substantially untruthfully, that you have already eaten?

Question 17 shows the determination to maintain the "supply" of starvation.

18. Have you ever regularly stolen or helped yourself to other people's sweets or food even though you had enough money to buy your own?

Question 18 is the same as for the *bingeing* questionnaire.

19. Do you find it difficult to finish everything on your plate, almost regardless of how little you put on it in the first place?

Question 19 shows that the "quantity" of starvation may on many occasions be more than planned.

20. Do you hate feeling full and find it virtually impossible to eat any more when you have that feeling?

Question 20 is the same question as question 19 expressed in more explicit form.

21. Do you find that you sometimes lose weight even though you were not specifically intending to do so?

Question 21 illustrates the inevitable physical consequence of starvation but demonstrates the surprise and pain that this can cause. The sufferer is caught between the demands of the addictive disease and the inevitable physical consequences.

22. Are you aware from your own experience that some substances act as "trigger" foods so that, once started, it is difficult to control further eating?

Question 22 is the same question as for the *bingeing* questionnaire and the examples given to illustrate a positive answer commonly demonstrate the craving for sugar and white flour.

23. Are you afraid that you will put on an *excessive* amount of weight if you give up smoking or using laxatives or appetite supressants or self-induced vomiting or exercising or give up strict control of food intake?

Question 23 is the same question as for the *bingeing* questionnaire and emphasises that most frustrating goal: "control". It is frustrating because control is not achievable by these methods.

24. If you go out in company to a restaurant do you prefer simply to drink some tea or coffee or have a diet drink while everyone else is eating?

Question 24 shows the adjustment of behaviour to fit anorexic values. The social engagement is accepted but not the eating process.

25. Have you ever had three or more different sizes of clothes in your adult, non-pregnant wardrobe.

Question 25 is the same question as for the *bingeing* questionnaire and observes the common consequences of all food addictions.

26. Has anyone else expressed repeated, serious, concern over your eating habits, body weight or shape?

Question 26 commonly receives the answer "yes", but the people who express the concern are resented and thought to be delusioned or obsessed (the very characteristics of the disease itself) because they are thought to be unjust and to lack understanding.

27. If you find that you have put on some weight do you commonly stop eating altogether for a day or two?

Question 27 illustrated that the "capacity" for starvation is enormous: it can be "switched on" with ease.

28. If you do eat in company do you like to be with special friends or family members whom you can rely upon to finish off some foods for you?

Question 28 shows that involving other people in maintaining one's capacity to continue one's particular behaviour is a classic addictive behaviour.

29. Do you find that all of these questions are perfectly straightforward and none of them a bit strange?

30. Do you feel you would instinctively understand someone who answered yes to *all* of these questions?

Questions 29 and 30 are the same as for the *bingeing* questionnaire and incidentally also for PROMIS Questionnaires on other addictions. All in all, the commonalities between all the Eating Disorders, and indeed all addictions, is considerable if not total. These separate Questionnaires are presented only for ease of identification while in a specific phase of Eating Disorder.

What are the common characteristics in any form of addictive disease?

Dr Richard Heilman of the Hazelden Foundation in Minnesota identifies the following eight characteristics:

1. *Pre-occupation.*
   Looking forward to use. Planning life around it. Making plans for specific times of abstinence.

2. *Use alone.*
   Use in private is just as comfortable (or even more so) as in company.

3. *Use for effect.*
   A special "lift", "feel" or "buzz" is sought from the substance or behaviour, rather than simply the taste or the normal consequence that is experienced by others.

4. *Use as a medicine.*
   The substance or behaviour may be used to help to relax or to help sleep or to provide stimulation or, most of all, to suppress uncomfortable emotional feelings.

5. *Protection of supply.*
   The substance or behaviour is used to smother disturbed feelings and its supply (or the money, time and other things required for it) tends to be disproportionately carefully protected.

6. *Using more than planned.*
   Incapacity to predict what will happen after the use of the substance or behaviour is started on any occasion.

7. *Increased capacity.*
   Greater capacity than others to use a particular substance or behaviour. In the late stages of the disease this "tolerance" is lost.

8. *Memory blankouts.*
   The memory functions of the brain may cease to function when it is intoxicated or otherwise overloaded. This may lead to loss of awareness that conversations or events ever took place. (This "denial" needs to be exposed by other people by *not* covering up the damaging consequences of use of the substance or behaviour).

Reflecting now upon the PROMIS Eating Disorders Questionnaires, it can be seen that these same characteristics (excluding the last) flow through the Questionnaires. Some questions look at one particular characteristic whereas other questions touch on several. There is considerable overlap between groups of questions concerning particular characteristics but in simple terms they correspond approximately as follows:

Questions 1 to 5	:	Preoccupation.
Questions 6 and 7	:	Use alone.
Questions 7 and 8	:	Use as a medicine.
Questions 9 to 12	:	Using for effect.
Questions 13 to 18	:	Protection of supply.

Questions 19 to 23 : Using more than planned.
Questions 24 to 28 : Higher capacity than others.

The eighth characteristic - memory blankouts - has been omitted from the PROMIS Eating Disorders Questionnaires despite the fact that some sufferers (in any phase) describe this experience as a result of either starving, binging or compulsive vomiting. The difficulty is in formulating a question that clearly delineates all eating disorder sufferers from other people.

Dr Heilman holds that addictive disease can only be diagnosed with certainty if four of these eight criteria are present. However, this really applies to live interviews with addiction counsellors rather than to written questionnaires which are easily fudged. The PROMIS Eating Disorders Questionnaires should therefore ideally be administered by an addiction counsellor who would put in further spontaneous questions in order to clarify the presence or absence of specific characteristics. Under those criteria it would possibly be reasonable to expect positive answers in four separate groups of questions corresponding to Dr Heilman's addiction characterstics.

However, it should be emphasised that the disease will split as many hairs as possible as well as flatly deny the obvious. After further interview with an addiction counsellor who specialises in eating disorders, it may be recommended that a period of in-patient assessment alongside other sufferers from eating disorders, would be the best method of being sure of diagnosis. The power of a group of sufferers to discern whether a newcomer truly belongs in the group or not is a far more accurate diagnostic tool than any written questionnaire or assessment by any individual addiction counsellor.

What is cross-addiction?

Any substance that tends to re-awaken the craving for the primary addictive "drug of choice" is cross-addictive with that drug of choice. Sufferers from eating disorders not infrequently have other forms of addictive disease.

Focussing attention upon individual sufferers and their capacity for *recovery* from addictive disease and providing general education on addictive disease and its recovery processes - rather than solely upon addictive substances or processes and their risks - is the best long term help for the individuals at risk of cross-addiction.

Early identification of those at risk from *any* form of addictive disease would be the best preventive measure of all.

What is physiological addiction?

Giving or taking repeated doses of any mood-altering substance, can result in the body becoming used to receiving that substance. Suddenly stopping the substance may result in acute "withdrawal" effects such as delirium tremens for alcohol or "cold turkey" (which feels like a bad bout of influenza) for heroin. Sudden withdrawal from sugar and white flour may cause headaches, dizziness and irritability. These physical effects of withdrawal indicate that the physical body craves for more of the drug and that it is physiologically addicted.

Cocaine or cannabis addiction does not invariably give rise to physiological addiction and there may be no significant physical effects of withdrawal. This can give rise to the mistaken belief that cocaine and cannabis are not addictive drugs. There can, however, be significant psychological effects of cocaine or cannabis use and there can be marked psychological effects of acute withdrawal.

The test of the addictive nature of a drug in a particular individual is not whether he or she can stop it but whether he or she can stay off it (and similar mood-altering drugs) indefinitely without any cravings to return.

Physiological addiction is not the same as addictive disease in which the sufferer finds himself or herself drawn back to the drug even against his or her will. It is often thought that alcoholism, drug addiction or the eating disorders are a failure of will-power and is evidence of a weak will or inadequate personality. This is not so.

People in recovery from various forms of addiction through Alcoholics, Narcotics or Overeaters Anonymous or other Anonymous Fellowships show no deficiency of will in comparison with the non-addictive population. If anything, while still using, they show the effects of excessive but futile use of strong will in trying to reduce or stop using alcohol or drugs or to follow strict diet or exercise regimes in order to gain control of their lives.?

Is it possible to predict which 10% of the population have addictive disease?

Addictive disease runs in families and it is therefore tempting to assume that up-bringing and family and social background are the prime cause of addictive disease. However, adoption studies where children of alcoholic parents have been brought up in non-alcoholic families show that genetic inheritance is a stronger predictor of addiction than is home or social background.

Sons of alcoholics are many times more likely to become alcoholics than are the sons of non-alcoholics.

An inherited predisposition to alcoholism has also been found in women and is evidently transmitted through the mother.

Sufferers from Chemical Dependency (Alcoholism or Drug Addiction) may have a specific abnormality in brain biochemistry. Compounds containing a particular amino acid, tryptophan, do not appear to be dealt with in quite the same way in the brain of a sufferer from addictive disease as they are in other people. A particular substance, tetra-hydro-iso-quinolone (THIQ), was thought at one time to be the active chemical "cause" of addiction but this is no longer thought to be the precise cause. A current theory is that in some individuals who have specific genetic predisposition, alcohol and other mood-altering drugs progressively act upon brain tissue and distort its biochemical function to produce abnormal chemicals similar to THIQ. These trigger the loss of control and obsession. Thus, addictive disease may be genetically predetermined but becomes progressively a disease of adaptation to the various damaging consequences of previous drinking or drug use.

Research work continues on various tryptophan-based products to see if there are such specific triggers. If there are, it may be possible in future years to identify potential sufferers from addictive disease through a simple blood test.

Research work also continues on scrotonin secretion by the brain and on drugs that may affect that process. The hope is that addictive disease of all kinds may be found to be due to a common biochemical dysfunction and that it can therefore be corrected. This simple physical concept of addictive disease and recovery has obvious superficial attraction but may be far from the full picture.

The question may then arise in the future as to what to do for those potential sufferers who are identified in this way and the answer is the same as for many families in whom there is other genetically inherited disease: specifically educate to protect. Practical advice for these specifically identified potential sufferers from addictive disease would include:

i. avoidance of intoxication or a specific "high" from any mood-altering substance or behaviour.

ii. awareness of the cross-addictive nature of many substances, including some specific foods and including mood-altering medications that are legally prescribed, dispensed or sold.

iii. awareness of the potentially addictive nature of some forms of behaviour or relationship.

It is appreciated that these recommendations may be difficult to accept but the ravages of addictive disease can be so severe that it must be sensible for those specifically at risk to be advised to do everything in their power to avoid awakening their potential.

Current educational programmes aimed at all school children on the risks of drug abuse or of eating disorders may fail to emphasise the major risks of alcohol and of some prescribed medicines and they may make the false assumptions that:

a. addiction is simply a product of repeated use rather than a specific risk of some particular individuals who have a tendency to addictive disease.

b. those who are specifically at risk from addictive disease will *believe* the evidence put to them on film or by teachers and adjust their behaviour accordingly. The fact is that they know from their own experience that many of their contemporaries take drugs occasionally or starve, binge or vomit on occasions and do not become addicted. They therefore tend to believe that they themselves also have minimal risk of addiction. The sufferers from eating disorders may believe that they are doing no more than their contemporaries in dieting, binging or vomiting and that they have minimal long term problems of addiction in a specific eating disorder. They will therefore tend to be sceptical about educational programmes on eating disorders or on drug addiction.

At least it can be said that these educational programmes may diminish the occasional experimental use of addictive drugs or processes (which may themselves be damaging or even fatal) by those who do not have addictive disease. But, for those who do have the tendency to addictive disease, the damage of awakening that disease has commonly already been done in Chemical Dependency (Drug Addiction and Alcoholism) by social, legal, alcohol and in the eating disorders by sugar and white flour.

CHAPTER **Two**

2. The Primary Disease

What sort of disease is the Primary Disease of Addiction?

The primary disease of any addiction – including any form of Eating Disorder – is a disease of the human spirit, of the sense of life, of hope, trust, love, faith and all the spiritual values.

It has consequences in mental, emotional and physical aspects of life. The mental and emotional consequences are frequently misdiagnosed as causes of the disease.

The spiritual values are not part of the intellect. Someone may be very unintelligent and yet have a good sense of hope or trust or love, whereas someone else who is highly intelligent may yet have a relatively poor facility in these senses.

Can recovery from any form of addictive disease be helped through encouragement or love?

Not in the customary manner of expression of encouragement or love. The disease comes from within and is not a reaction to outside circumstances or people. Only "tough love" is helpful, loving the sufferer but allowing him or her to take the full consequences of all actions caused by the disease. This helps to break through the defensive "denial system" and encourages the sufferer to seek truly effective help.

The sufferer has to want to seek help and will not want to do so if other people cover up the consequences of addictive disease.

Whatever the sufferer or family member may say at times of anger or despair, nobody causes addictive disease or can control it or cure it. It is not caused by the absence of encouragement or love, nor prevented or helped by their presence.

Regardless of encouragement or love (or hostility or punishment), the disease progresses and, in the absence of treatment through the appropriate Anonymous Fellowship for each form of addiction, is commonly fatal. Thus, Alcoholism is treated through Alcoholics

Anonymous, Drug addiction through Narcotics Anonymous, Compulsive Gambling through Gamblers Anonymous, the eating disorders through Overeaters, Bulimics or Anorexics Anonymous and so on. In each case the primary addictive disease of the human spirit is identical whereas the route through which it expresses itself may vary. In some people it appears to be channeled through one particular form of addiction. In others it may express itself through several. It is not known whether all or only some sufferers from addictive disease find that their addictive disease can switch itself from one addiction to another. Whatever is the case, addictive disease in any form can be helped (if at all) through the Anonymous Fellowships and it is not specifically helped through encouragement or love or for that matter through education or punishment.

Many processes may be helpful alongside treatment for the primary addictive disease in the Anonymous Fellowships, but none without it.

The earlier in the progress of the disease that "tough love" is practised then the earlier will the sufferer be likely to seek recovery and, hopefully, the less damaging will have been the consequences.

What are the consequences of any form of addictive disease?

Spiritual: The sufferer loses a sense of faith, trust, hope and love in himself or herself, in other people and in any form of benevolent God. As a result of this loss of belief in the potential for good in the future, the sufferer comes to perceive himself or herself as having few choices of action in life. The general sense of well-being in life is lost.

Emotional: The sufferer may have significant mood swings, tending always towards depression resulting from the damaged sense of hope and other damaged senses. When the only choice appears to be between continuing depression or continuing the various problems associated with addictive disease, it is small wonder that sufferers from Chemical Dependency (drug addiction and alcoholism) alone constitute 30% of those people who commit suicide. Other forms of addiction bring many more suicides. Anorexia itself could be described as a form of slow suicide. Addictive disease in general has a fearful mortality from this cause alone.

Alcohol and other drugs including sugar and white flour have direct sedative and stimulant effects upon the brain, both acting at the same time but over different periods of time. The initial sedative effect causes sleep but the sufferer is wide awake early the next morning from the longer-acting stimulant effect. The consequent mix of anxiety and depression both in the short term and in the long term is frequently misdiagnosed as Manic Depression.

Behavioural: Previous values change as the sufferer becomes increasingly in the grip of the disease. Old friendships are broken and replaced by new friends who find the new behavioural patterns more tolerable. Commonly these new friendships are with other sufferers from the same addiction or with people who have addictive disease in their close family. Progressively more of the sufferer's behaviour is determined by the eight addictive characteristics described by Dr Richard Heilman and outlined in Chapter 1.

Social: Addiction of any kind is a disease of isolation. It is not just that the sufferer loses friends from the disordered behaviour. Remarkably, it is commonly the sufferer himself or herself who breaks off social relationships and activities because of a feeling of not being properly appreciated or understood. There is an inner sense of alienation from his or her own true self and from others.

Legal: Recurrent problems with the Law are commonplace in Chemical Dependency but less so in the eating disorders. However, people suffering from compulsive overeating or bulimia may steal food and gradually change their legal values along with other values as their addictive disease progresses.

By contrast, sufferers from anorexia may be so law-binding and "perfect" – in every way other than in their relationship with food – that it becomes difficult to confront them on the issue of food. It almost seems unfair to "criticise" them over this "little" thing – or at any rate that is what the addictive disease would have us believe. This is an example of control of other people through the passivity that is a basic feature of anorexia.

Marital: Marital problems are almost inevitable. Life alongside someone suffering from any form of addiction can become intolerable. In Chemical Dependency this is fairly obvious but sufferers from the Eating Disorders can be no less intolerant and intolerable. As the eight characteristics of addictive disease progressively bite into the sufferer so he or she progressively bites into food (or in anorexia progressively refuses to bite at all) and also, metaphorically, bites into his or her close relationships.

Professional: In Chemical Dependency and other addictions, including compulsive overeating and bulimia, the trail of broken promises at home is mirrored by a trail of broken contracts at work. Divorce at home may be mirrored by changes of work or even of occupation. The work record becomes progressively worse. Absenteeism, recurrent minor illnesses, accidents at home and at work and disturbed relationships with colleagues are all commonplace. However, most sufferers from addictive disease are nonetheless in full employment and often they cling desperately to that employment while progressively losing everything else of value in their lives.

The exception is the sufferer from anorexia, aptly described by Dr Steven Levenkron as "The best little girl in the world" in a book of that name published by Warner Books. But in anorexia the sufferer may become progressively more obsessive and this will affect the quality of work. Ultimately he or she may become too weak to work at all.

Intellectual: There is some evidence of "state-dependent learning" which results in the brain being best able to recall factual information and practical skills when it is in the same state as when that information was first learnt or skill first practised. Thus, the student who regularly uses alcohol or cannabis, sugar or caffeine or nicotine in times of study may have poor recall if he or she has no cannabis or alcohol, sugar or caffeine or nicotine at the time of an examination. Correspondingly, some practical skills, such as playing sports, may have to be re-learnt when sober or non-tranquillised if they were first learnt under the influence of alcohol or drugs and this may possibly apply also to sugar and caffeine and nicotine.

It is small wonder that the sufferer from addictive disease comes to believe that his or her body and mind actually benefits from the use of the particular drug or behaviour of choice. But the long-term effects upon the brain are to dull its critical faculties and to impair its capacity for memory and accuracy. Fortunately, much of this is reversible in recovery.

Educational: Most examinations are tests of short term memory and this is exactly what is damaged in alcohol or drug use. Some high achievers survive high alcohol consumption for many years but the damaging effects of drugs tend to be quicker in their tendency to cause intellectual impairment.

In the Eating Disorders the withdrawal of sugar may cause dizziness and light headedness, irritability and difficulty in concentration. The same symptoms may occur if sugar is suddenly introduced after a period of starvation. Consequently, there can be educational consequences as a result of the irregular eating pattern of an eating disorder.

Financial: The progressive effect of Chemical Dependency or any other form of addictive disease is loss of one thing after another: occupation, home, friends, family, possessions and finally life itself. Throughout all of this progressive loss the increasing financial insecurity tortures the spirit and degrades each day, month or year more than the last.

Progressive effects of eating disorders can follow exactly this pattern. The sufferers may become progressively more isolated as food comes to occupy the central position in life. Again, high achievers may survive for many years but it is noticable that people who are excessively fat or excessively thin often have difficulty in obtaining and maintaining full employment. Sufferers from bulimia may find it difficult to concentrate upon their work and, as a result, may lose their employment. Sufferers from compulsive overeating or Bulimia may spend considerable sums of money on binges. This can be exceedingly distressing financially as well as spiritually, particularly if the binge is followed by self-induced vomiting.

Physical: Every system of the body is progressively damaged.

In compulsive overeating the body gets progressively fatter and heavier from deposition of fat in the tissues. Most of this fat is stored in specific fat cells under the skin or in other tissues such as the omentum (a form of internal apron in the abdomen) but it is also deposited in other tissues and organs such as the muscles, liver and heart so that they became weaker. Control of sugar metabolism by the pancreas becomes less efficient so that there is a tendency to diabetes.

The arteries throughout the whole body build up fat deposits inside their linings and tend to "fur up" like water pipes. This leads to major risks when the arteries become blocked altogether. Blockage in the coronary arteries supplying the muscle wall of the heart causes heart attacks and blockage in the cerebral arteries supplying the brain tissue causes strokes, leading to paralysis of one side of the body or the other. Many heart attacks and strokes are fatal. Although the death certificate commonly simply records "coronary thrombosis" or "cerebral thromboses", the true original cause may have been compulsive overeating or nicotine addiction or both.

The effect of significant increase in weight, coupled with lack of physical fitness, leads to strain on the muscles and joints. The extra weight causes the joints of the spine and of the hips and legs to be under very considerable pressure and, over the years, the joint tissues progressively and painfully wear out.

Weakness in the abdominal muscles lead to herniae and increased abdominal pressure leads to haemorrhoids.

The increase in fat tissue causes tranquillising effects upon the brain, ultimately leading to Pickwickian Syndrome, in which excessively fat people find it difficult not only to move about but even to stay awake.

In bulimia the regurgitated hydrochloric acid from the stomach burns the tissues of the oesophagus (gullet) and progressively erodes the enamel of the teeth. The perpetual loss of acid also causes severe problems with body metabolism: the biochemical control of body acidity and alkalinity becomes seriously deranged. The sufferer may look relatively normal to the outside world, being neither excessively fat nor thin, but internally there is chaos.

In anorexia the progressive effects of starvation affect all the tissues of the body. The external appearance becomes emaciated as first the fat stores are depleted and later the muscle tissues themselves are progressively broken down to provide biochemical fuel. The body progressively eats itself from within. The balance of various body fluids and elemental constituents becomes disturbed so that potassium ions in particular become depleted and this has serious effects upon conductivity of nerve impulses and on the electrical conductivity of heart tissues. Vitamin deficiency can lead to the various deficiency syndromes. Menstural cycles commonly cease. The skin becomes delicate and covered with fine "lanugo" hair as on a new-born baby.

Many of these physical complications are reversible once the prime cause of the damage – overeating, recurrent vomiting or starving – is discontinued: the human body has amazing capacity to repair itself. But enormous numbers of sufferers from the eating disorders, which are treatable conditions, die of these secondary physical consequences while their primary addictive disease remains undiagnosed or inappropriately treated.

What are the phases of addictive disease?

The early phase is characterised by increased tolerance to the substance or process of addiction and the sufferer feels better for its use.

The middle phase is where this tolerance is progressively lost so that there is decreased control over use and over associated behaviour. There is decreased ability to stay away from the first use in any day of the substance or process of addiction.

The chronic phase shows progressive deterioration in emotional stability so that relationships become progressively damaged. Intellectual function is damaged so that thought processes and the capacity to instill any form of order into personal and professional life progressively deteriorates. At this time the primary need perceived by the sufferer is to protect the future capacity to use the addictive substance or behaviour and this dependence results in changes in beliefs and values. Reality becomes so painful that the sufferer uses his or her substance or process of addiction in order to survive the emotional carnage. As previously described, "state dependent learning" occurs when the brain will repeat learned functions only when in the same "drugged" state as when the subject matter or practical activity was first learnt. Repeated use of the particular addictive substance or behaviour is perceived as necessary for emotional and even physical survival, yet at the same time it contributes to further decline.

What are the personality traits of Addictive Disease?

Conflict with authority: The sufferer genuinely believes that he or she is normal and that the world has problems and so do the people who "run" the world.

Criticism of others: The sufferer believes that if only *other* people would change then everything would be all right. Blaming other people, while opting out of responsibility for his or her own condition, is the hallmark of a sufferer from addictive disease.

Intellectualisation: There is nothing that the disease likes more than a circuitous argument in search of absolute proof on precise definitions of addiction. Feelings are suppressed while the head endlessly debates.

Anger and Resentment: Anger is so fundamental to addictive disease that it goes with the person rather than with specific events.

Stubbornness: The disease is closed-minded and not open to persuasion. Why should it be? – *Other* people are perceived to have the problem; *not* the sufferer.

Self-centredness: Individual willpower, the absolute determination to control the addictive substance or behaviour, is exactly what keeps the disease going. This emphasis on control, despite all the evidence that this is precisely what is being progressively lost, focusses the sufferer's mind all the time on self and not upon others. The sufferer becomes the total centre of his or her own world, regardless of relationships with others in the past or in the future.

Pride: Determined belief in the capacity for self control results in pride that the sufferer has special standards and abilities that others lack. This exaggeration of the sufferer's ability is in compensation for the inner lack of belief in self.

Procrastination: The continuing need to demonstrate self control results in all lesser activities being put off for the time being.

Self pity: The spiritual isolation, the feeling that the sufferer is "special and different" from other people and misunderstood by them, results in recurrent thoughts of victimisation.

Perfectionism: The reason so many things are delayed is that they *have* to be perfect. Criticising other people for their inadequacies puts a tremendous burden of perfectionism on the sufferer in his or her own activities.

Externalisation: The poor internal self-image is reflected outwards on to other people and on to external circumstances rather than being recognised as the diseased part of self.

Denial: The fixed belief that the sufferer may have problems and that these may be a cause of the recourse to substances or behaviours of addiction but certainly *not* a consequence of them, is the central psycho-pathology of the disease. This denial is so certain in the mind of the sufferer that other people close to the sufferer may even come to doubt their own certainty that there really are problems or they may even come to doubt their own sanity.

Is addictive disease a real disease and should doctors waste valuable time on something that is usually considered to be self-induced?

Doctors spend enormous amounts of time on the consequences of addictive disease in the sufferer and in family members and (in Industrial Medicine) in problems at work. Spending time considering that addictive disease might be the true cause of many of these secondary consequences is a better use of the doctor's time than trying to tidy up the same repeated consequences time and time again.

Although the physical act of using a substance or process of addiction is technically self-induced, the spiritual disease that leads to this compulsion is a disease that has clearly identifiable characteristics and outcomes, that runs in families and may even be genetically inherited (this does not mean that if your parents have addictive disease then you will necessarily also have addictive disease, but it does mean that there is a higher chance of your having it) and therefore the existence of the disease may be totally beyond the control of the sufferer.

Cancers, infections and medical and surgical conditions are not the only "real" diseases. Doctors already spend large amounts of time on conditions – such as bereavement and unemployment – that have significant medical consequences, on contraception, short sight and similar conditions that are not "real" diseases at all and on the common cold which is frequently mis-named influenza and which requires no treatment at all.

Heart attacks and lung cancer are directly linked with cigarette smoking which is sometimes but not always due to nicotine addiction. A multitude of medical conditions are due to being over-weight which in many people may be simply the consequence of self indulgence rather than food addiction.

Many accidents are caused by sports or by other activities whose risks are well known.

The acceptance of these conditions as being worthy of medical time, and the tendency to resent scarce resources being used on addictive disease of one kind or another, have more to do with fear or disgust than whether or not a condition is demonstrably self-induced.

As an ideal general principle, doctors do not moralise but simply deal with the medical condition or consequence in the patient in front of them. However, because of their own fear or disgust and the general lack of understanding of addictive disease, this reluctance to moralise is frequently forgotten.

A fundamental clinical maxim is to listen to the patient. Sufferers from addictive disease say "I have tried repeatedly to give up but I find that I cannot. I am always drawn back to it as if I was under a compulsion." They are telling the truth.

The progression of understanding of various forms of disease can be traced throughout history:

Short sight may not have been understood by stone-age man. Entrusted to look after the fire or the children, let alone to go hunting, the myopic savage would have been a menace to group security. There may have been no understanding whatever of the concept of not being able to see as well as other people. Nowadays we fully accept short sight. It limits some occupations but we have no thought that it significantly affects personality, trustworthiness or sanity.

Diabetes leads to increased sugar in the blood and this can lead to confusion and coma. This will certainly have caused concern in the Middle Ages and some unfortunates may have been considered to be "possessed" of evil spirits and treated accordingly. Nowadays, diabetes is understood and in general is accepted even though hypoglycaemic (too little sugar in the blood) attacks, from taking too much insulin relative to body requirements, can result in strange behaviour which may at times have tragic consequences, as indeed can misdiagnosis (usually as drunkenness) from hyperglycaemia (too much sugar in the blood) in untreated diabetes. Nonetheless, one would not generally fear someone with diabetes, nor be unduly concerned to employ someone who has diabetes or be worried if one's daughter were to consider marrying such a person.

Epilepsy, despite the known medical facts that it commonly "burns out" after ten years and that it is not normally associated with disorders of personality, nonetheless still causes considerable concern in society. Many people are reluctant to employ someone who has epilepsy and they might be very concerned if their daughter intended to marry such a person. The situation is not helped by the writers of "soap operas" who "explain" the behaviour of a murderer, child molester or other deviant by saying that he or she had epilepsy or a brain tumour. Epilepsy may be understood today but it is a long way from being accepted in the same way as diabetes, let alone short sight.

Addictive disease is simply the next in the progression from short sight to diabetes and on to epilepsy. It is neither understood nor accepted today and is greatly feared. In time it will be both understood and accepted as a disease that is not the fault of the sufferer and from which full recovery is possible.

What does it feel like to have addictive disease?

Confusing: A sufferer may be highly intelligent, have a responsible job, be very caring and concerned for his or her family and yet still be drawn by this compulsion to use his or her drug or behaviour of choice and, as a result, progressively to destroy everything of value.

Frightening: Sufferers are repeatedly shown the potential consequences by doctors and others but "in denial" do not understand or accept the connection between the use of their substance or behaviour of addiction and these fearful consequences. When, ultimately, they fail in their efforts to give up they become exceedingly fearful and ashamed and may even believe themselves to be insane. Many commit suicide because they see no possible hope for the future.

Lonely: The spiritual isolation of the disease is lonely enough but add to this the "Jekyll and Hyde" behaviour (depending upon whether or not the substance or behaviour of addiction has been used that day) causing untold damage to family and other relationships and the loneliness becomes intense. This loneliness then tends to be misdiagnosed as depression and medications may be prescribed which may make the disease even worse. The external arrogance or bonhomie of the primary sufferer may be no more than a fearful mask.

How can Addiction of one kind or another justifiably be called a "Spiritual" Disease?

Because the primary disease leads to a disorder of mood with a poor self image and a sense of shame and unworthiness. It is this disorder of the human spirit that leads the sufferer to seek mood-altering substances or behaviours.

Because it gets better with the "spiritual" treatment of the Anonymous Fellowhsips. Meetings of these Anonymous Fellowships can be described but precisely why the process works is not known in scientific terms. Similarly, science may describe what electricity, gravity or radiation do and we can use them reliably in practical applications, but we still may not be able to describe precisely what they *are*.

Because sufferers feel better and are temporarily relieved of their urge to use an addictive substance or behaviour after a meeting of an appropriate Anonymous Fellowship. Involvement in a meeting is a "spiritual" process: it is not simply mental, educational, emotional nor the process of providing group support, although there are elements of all of these. Essentially, active involvement in a meeting reverses the characteristics of the disease, giving a sense of peace, hope, trust, love and other positive senses. Repeated involvement in meetings leads to progressive erosion of the personality traits of the disease. Discontinuation of involvement in meetings leads to their recurrence.

It is not primarily a mental disease because thought processes return to being perfectly intact in those who are in substantial recovery through the Anonymous Fellowships. Thus, the "stinking thinking" of addictive disease is reversible.

It does not respond to other forms of mental or emotional treatment such as analytical psychotherapy, behaviour therapy or general psychiatric group therapy, although any of these may possibly be helpful in dealing with other issues once the primary disease is in recovery through the Anonymous Fellowships.

It has consequences in other aspects of life but treating these consequences has no effect on the primary "spiritual" disease. Frequently, the consequences are misdiagnosed and treated as causes but this is no more justified than asking an educational psychologist to treat the disturbed thought processes of someone in pain from acute gout.

When the primary "spiritual" disease is treated through the Anonymous Fellowships the consequences of addictive disease gradually resolve.

Why are other concepts on the cause of addiction inaccurate?

Adoption studies show that nature is a stronger predictor of addictive disease than nurture.

Addictive disease affects sufferers throughout the whole of society and is not related to social class, income, employment or privilege or lack of privilege of any kind.

There is no evidence that stress causes addiction as such although a stressful life event may trigger latent addictive disease. Many individuals and families have significant stresses yet do not develop addictive disease. Conversely, there may be addictive disease in individuals and families in which there is apparently very considerable financial and emotional privilege rather than any obvious stress. The concepts of "perceived" or "relative" stress may then sometimes be used to justify adherence to a theory of stress causing addiction - but, by this time, the stress argument is wearing thin.

Addictive disease varies in intensity from one individual to another in the same way as short sight varies from one individual to another. Thus, genetic inheritance may be variable rather than absolute in its effects in different people and the presence or absence of addictive disease may be more correctly a matter of degree.

There is no evidence that disturbed upbringing leads to an increased incidence of addictive disease. In families in which one or both parents have addictive disease there will, of course, be disturbed up-bringing but the cause of addictive disease in any of the children appears more likely to be genetic because there is no increased incidence of addictive disease in children brought up in disturbed environments where the parents did not have addictive disease.

Studies of the behaviour of people recovering from addictive disease through Alcoholics Anonymous in wartime and under similar severe stress show a better capacity to withstand stress (probably through long practice) than in the general population.

There is no evidence that addiction develops merely as a result of excessive use. Many sufferers from addictive disease describe their very first exposure to a mood-altering substance or behaviour as being a special, profound, experience. They state their belief that they were aware of a special relationship with that substance or behaviour from then onwards. Nonetheless, it is true that the addiction is to mood-alteration rather than simply to the substance or behaviour and that, as tolerance develops, progressively more of the substance or behaviour is required to produce the mood-altering effect.

Conversely, there are many people who drink excessively and get drunk repeatedly or who go through a phase of drug use, gambling, cigarette smoking, bingeing or enforced vomiting or other behaviour that may be similar to that of addictive disease but they can nonetheless stop these processes when they decide to do so and not be inexorably drawn back to that primary substance or behaviour. They do not have addictive disease: they may simply have become physiologically addicted so that their bodies and minds have become temporarily habituated to a particular substance or behaviour. On ceasing it they may suffer some physical withdrawal effects but will not be inexorably drawn back to the primary substance or behaviour. Their behaviour may have been self-indulgent rather than compulsive or addictive. There is no direct evidence that *all* people have the potential for addictive disease within them and, conversely, there is evidence that addictive disease seems only to affect particular people, albeit an enormous number.

There is no evidence that addictive disease arises from traumas of early childhood or that psycho-therapeutic techniques that explore the emotional and behavioural patterns established in these early years have any effect whatever in the understanding or treatment of addictive disease. They may well provide insight and help for other behavioural disorders but not for addictive disease as such. Thus, one would advise sufferers to deal first with their addictive disease through 12 Step programme of recovery through the Anonymous Fellowships and later, while in the second stage of recovery, come to deal with other behavioural issues through whatever method may be individually appropriate.

Alcoholics Anonymous describe Alcoholism as being a physical allergy allied to a mental obsession, giving rise to a threefold illness: ". . . we have been not only mentally and physically ill, we have been spiritually sick." This description fits the observable characteristics and progress of addictive disease, although it might be more appropriate to substitute the social term "sensitivity" for the strictly clinical term "allergy".

The Psychiatrist, Dr William Glasser, author of "Reality Therapy" and "Control Theory" holds that the search for unconditional love is at the heart of addictive disease. His understanding is as follows: Blaming others for the condition of self is the psychological origin of the disease. There may nonetheless be a genetic predisposition that leads to the mood altering substance providing the perceived perfect solution to this quest for unconditional love. However, other people do not accept the sufferer's determination that mood-altering substances or behaviour are the solution to problems rather than a further cause of them. Consequently, the sufferer increasingly cuts himself or herself off from the reality of life as presented by others and continues to blame them for their failure to provide unconditional love and "understanding" comparable to that experienced in the relationship with the substances or behaviour that lead to alteration of mood. Ultimately this relationship with mood-altering substances or behaviour is the only relationship left.

Control Theory holds that the sufferer has the choice of "pictures" of perception in his or her mind giving images of how life "should" be. Illness occurs when these pictures are refused the opportunity to conform with pictures of life as it actually is. The sufferer attempts to gain control by changing his or her pictures of reality to conform to the pictures of perception of how life should be. Reality Therapy involves confronting the sufferer with the reality of life as perceived by others

(Excerpt from p. 64 of "Alcoholics Anonymous" reprinted with permission of Alcoholics Anonymous World Services, Inc.)

and helping him or her gradually to change the perception of how life should be so that it comes nearer to how life actually is. Thus, alcohol (and other mood-altering substances) come to be seen in reality as mood-altering chemicals rather than solely as a perceived solution to problems. Futher, Control Theory and Reality Therapy dictate that ultimately the sufferer is himself or herself responsible for changing the pictures in his or her own perceptions. The sufferer has to learn to live in reality, blaming self rather than others for his or her own problems and recognising that unconditional love could only be received when it is equally freely given.

These concepts of Dr Glasser fit closely with the experience and understanding of the Anonymous Fellowships and with the practical treatment methods employed by treatment centres based upon their principles. Unconditional love is precisely what is given and received in the Anonymous Fellowships and the application of reality as the standard by which sufferers need to live serves gradually to clear away the confusion caused by addictive disease. The Anonymous Fellowships help sufferers to come to recognise that their problems lie primarily in their own perceptions and behaviour and that solutions lie in giving help to others and asking for help from them.

What is the normal course of progression of addictive disease?

Compulsive overeating, like alcoholism, may progress quickly over a few years but commonly progresses over twenty years or even more from first binge or intoxication until terminal chronic disease.

Bulimia and anorexia, like addiction to drugs, may progress more rapidly over three to five years although they can in some sufferers take much longer.

Different people have different severity of addictive disease.
Compare X, Y, Z. in fig (i)

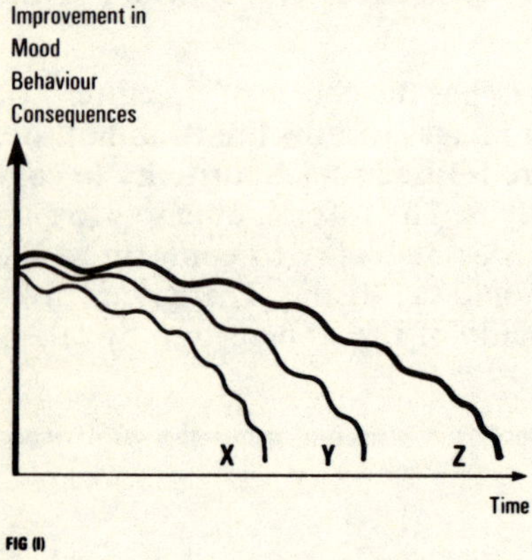

FIG (I)

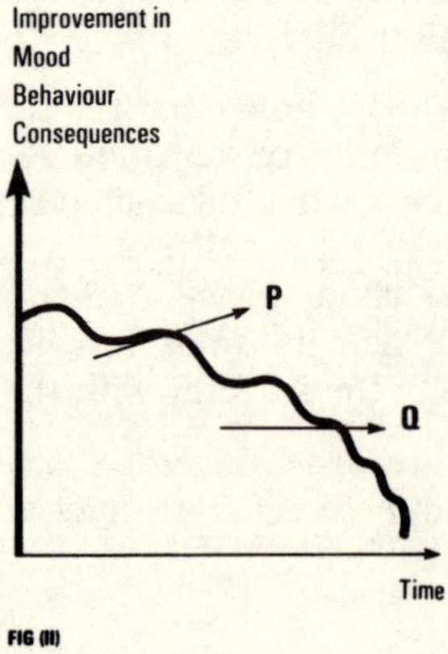

FIG (II)

In some the progression is very rapid while in others it takes very many years and may only be triggered by an acute personal crisis such as retirement or when the children leave home (the "empty nest syndrome").

The gradual decline and progressively more severe consequences are not predictable. They come and go and there will be times of definite improvement (see P in fig (ii)). These times are used by the sufferer to prove to self and others that he or she has no problem with addictive disease but is in full control, provided that outside circumstances do not cause further upset. The family and others also cling to these times of false hope.

But the time comes when control is lost again and on each occasion the disease and its consequences are worse than previously. Each new pit is deeper than the one before. (compare 1, 2, 3 in fig (iii)).

The time between successive pits becomes progressively shorter (compare A with B in fig (iv)).

The disease accelerates so that the times of improvement become no longer measurable improvements but simply times of no further drastic decline (see Q in fig (ii)) . . . until the next time.

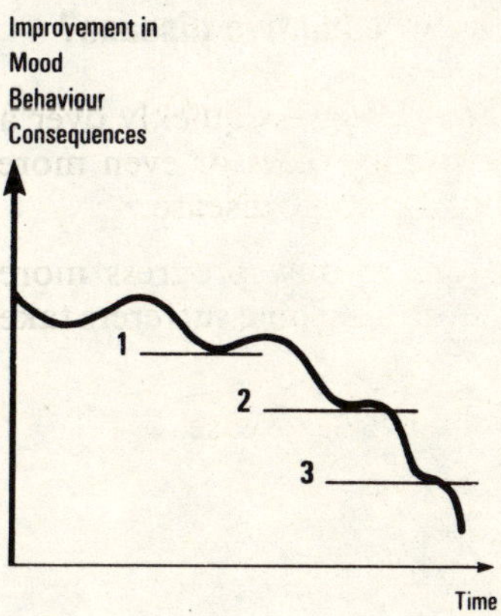

FIG (III)

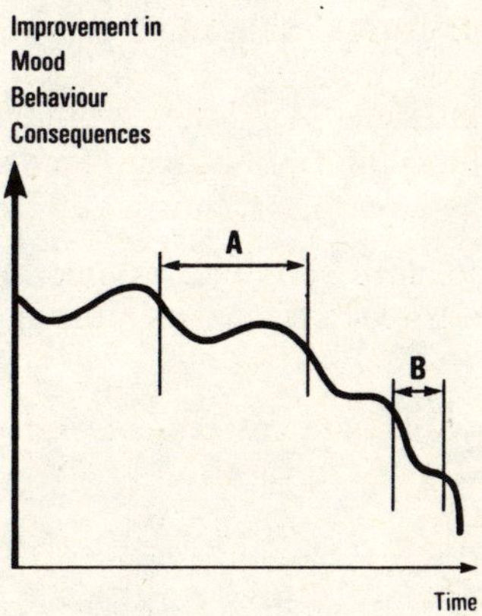

FIG (IV)

Addictive disease, primarily affecting at least ten per cent of the population and secondarily affecting the lives of maybe three times as many, is amongst the most common of all conditions. We tend not to be aware of it except in its final stages and because of commonly ambivalent attitudes towards alcohol, sugar and white flour, "soft" drugs and prescribed medicines. We may believe that because most people find it possible to use alcohol or food harmlessly all other people should also be able to do so. We may also believe that nobody but "rock musicians" and "media people" take drugs and that only fashion models, ballet dancers and air hostesses have eating disorders. We may further believe that medical prescriptions for minor tranquillisers and sleeping tablets, particularly for ourselves, are only reasonable. All these beliefs are ill advised.

Through its consequences, addictive disease of one kind or another is a major cause of disturbance in human relationships and it is probably the foremost of all killing diseases with a fearful mortality rate in the untreated disease. It is so common and so devastating that we tend to be blinded by it and do not see it.

CHAPTER **Three**

3. Other Addictions

In addition to the Eating Disorders, what other addictions are there?

Chemical Dependency (Alcoholism and Drug Addiction.)

Addiction to other drugs such as nicotine and caffeine.

Gambling and other forms of risk taking.

Addictive relationships.

Compulsive exercise taking, workaholism, compulsive over spending and similar behavioural addictions.

What is the nature of Chemical Dependency (Alcoholism and Drug Addiction) and what are the consequences?

An alcoholic is:

Someone who cannot predict what will happen after he or she takes the first drink. The alcoholic may be able to do without a drink for days, weeks, months or even years but, once he or she takes the first drink in any day, there is no prediction of when that drinking bout will stop. It may stop after one or two drinks or it may go on into a spree. "Inability to predict what will happen after taking the first drink" is how we define alcoholism.

Alcohol is an addictive drug to some people: probably to about 10% of the population and probably not to the other 90%. This figure varies in different cultures.

There are common false assumptions:

that all tramps are alcoholic and all sufferers from alcoholism are tramps.

that sufferers from alcoholism get drunk easily.

that sufferers from alcoholism always drink in the mornings.

that sufferers from alcoholism cannot stop drinking for a day, a week, a month, a year or more.

that you cannot be alcoholic if you still have a family, a house, a car, a job and money in the bank.

that you cannot be alcoholic unless you are first a regular heavy drinker.

that alcoholism occurs in people who are weak-willed or morally degenerate or both.

The consequences of alcohol consumption in the UK are:

i. "8–14 million working days a year are lost through heavy drinking".

Alcohol Concern.

ii. "The total annual cost of alcohol misuse is £1.9 billion, including £748 million cost of sickness absence".

Professor Alan Maynard, Department of Health and Economics, University of York.

iii. Alcohol abuse is associated with:
52% of deaths from fire.
66% of attempted suicides.
62% of serious head injuries in males.
45% of fatal road accidents involving young people.
36% of road traffic accidents involving pedestrians.
33% of all domestic accidents.
30% of drownings.
30% of all accidents not involving road traffic.

Summary researched by "Action on Alcohol Abuse".

What is cross-addiction?

Any substance that tends to re-awaken the craving for the primary addictive "drug of choice" is cross-addictive with that drug of choice. Many substances that are mood-altering are "cross-addictive" with alcohol.

Each sufferer from addictive disease tends to have one favourite "drug of choice" that is particularly craved although some sufferers may have two or more "drugs of choice" that are equally craved. Other "secondary" drugs of choice are cross-addictive because they have similar but not such marked effects as the primary drug of choice for that particular sufferer.

Alcohol tends to be cross-addictive with other mood-altering chemicals such as minor tranquillisers, anti-depressants, sleeping tablets and some other prescribed drugs such as Pethidine, Morphia and many other pain-killers, anti-histamines and the various illegal drugs such as cannabis, amphetamines, LSD, Mescalin, Ecstasy, magic mushrooms and other hallucinogens, cocaine, heroin and opium.

A sufferer from alcoholism given any one of these cross-addictive substances will tend to revert to using his primary drug of choice, alcohol.

Extreme care must therefore be taken in the medicinal use of any of these drugs in sufferers from alcoholism.

It also follows that any sufferer primarily addicted to one of these other drugs will probably be cross-addicted to alcohol. For example, a sufferer from heroin addiction in recovery is best advised to be totally abstinent from alcohol: the risks of cross-addiction are great.

It should be borne in mind that despite the fact that psychiatric diseases such as depression or manic-depression tend to be vastly over-diagnosed, particularly in sufferers from alcoholism in whom these features may be indications of their primary disease of alcoholism, some patients do have both addictive disease and psychiatric disease and need appropriate treatment for both. The incidence of true psychiatric disease in patients with addictive disease is no greater than in the general population.

What cross-addictions are particularly common in sufferers from eating disorders?

Chemical Dependency is a frequent cross-addiction, most commonly with alcohol or tranquillisers.

Compulsive overspending. Some treatment centres specialising in eating disorders find the need to take a significant number of patients to meetings of Debtors Anonymous.

Compulsive overexercising. Sufferers from anorexia and bulimia may have major problems with overexercising and may feel exceedingly deprived if disallowed the use of a gymnasium. Conversely, the compulsive overeater may have to be encouraged to the point of coercion to use the gymnasium or take any other form of physical exercise at all. Some treatment centres have a policy of grouping eating disorder patients in threes – one from each type of eating disorder – so that social activities, such as walking around the grounds, are performed at an average pace and each sufferer comes to recognise his or her own potential for extremes of activity through observing the activity of peers.

Compulsive sexual activity. It is not unusual for sufferers from bulimia or compulsive overeating to go through a phase of promiscuity. Sexual abuse in early childhood is a common feature in many sufferers from eating disorders. It might be that early childhood trauma of any kind could be the stimulus that awoke the addictive potential and that food was the only available drug of choice at that time.

How does one know if someone is on drugs?

The behavioural consequences of drug use are virtually the same as for alcohol or for eating disorders.

Drugs such as cannabis specifically affect short-term memory and therefore under-achievement in examinations and other tests is a common indicator, although care must be taken not to assume that all under-achievers are necessarily on drugs.

By observing progressive disrespect for reliability and dependability, personal appearance, legal and other authority and for social pursuits and friendships that are not alcohol or drug related. Again, some of these processes occur in normal adolescence and indeed even all of them may occur in some people in the absence of drug use, although this is improbable. It should be emphasised that occasional drug use may be simply a "normal" pattern of behaviour corresponding to "normal" drunkenness and not necessarily be a sign of delinquency, depravity or addictive disease. Nonetheless, disrespect for the law and general customs of society are commonly a positive sign of addictive disease. On the other hand there are some sufferers from addictive disease - particularly cocaine users - who may for quite some time be highly respectable and law-abiding and thereby wrongly assume that they are not addicted.

By looking for specific physical signs, such as the "nodding" head of heroin users, the lack of general motivation in cannabis users, acute wildness in amphetamine or cocaine users or slowness in barbiturate or tranquilliser users, may all be totally unrewarding. Addictive drugs are commonly used in combination and the users become temporarily "expert" on the pharmacological effects of drugs and at balancing the effects of one drug with those of another. Further, these general behavioural characteristics can easily be confused with those of normal adolescence or personal idiosyncracy and, conversely, one may find much "normal" behaviour even in those who have severe addictive disease. Paradoxically, families are often more concerned by the behaviour of a primary sufferer who, unbeknown to them, is desperately trying to withdraw from drugs than they are by his or her apparently normal behaviour when he or she is continuing regular use.

The discovery of tablets, syringes, strips of silver foil, small folded paper envelopes, strange pipes and various other items of paraphernalia associated with drug use may be no more than an indication of experiment rather than addiction. Further, the repeated searching and worrying is intolerable and utterly destructive of normal family life and in any case it is not helpful in either preventing or in treating addictive disease.

The discovery that someone knows a great deal about the effects of drugs and has strong opinions or whether or not a particular drug or process is or is not addictive is a strong positive indicator of addictive disease. The rest of the population, including many members of the medical profession, are simply not all that interested in drugs or in addiction to the extent of such preoccupation.

None of these individual factors is proof of addiction but any of them can be a cause for concern and a repeated pattern of one or more factors is an indication that professional assessment is indicated.

Are other addictions real addictions?

Yes, and they have real consequences.

For all substances and behaviour of addiction the primary nature of addictive potential lies in the individual and not simply in the substance or behaviour.

Some people can take or leave cigarettes just as they can take or leave an alcoholic drink. Others find that however hard they try to stop smoking and however much they may be aware of the damaging consequences of continuing to do so, they simply cannot stop but find themselves compelled to continue. These people have addictive disease and their drug of choice is nicotine.

The same can happen for some people with caffeine, which is found particularly in coffee, tea, cocoa, chocolate and in smaller quantities in lemonade, cola and similar soft drinks.

The physical consequences of nicotine addiction (and of nicotine use, irrespective of addiction) are well known and dramatic but nontheless frequently denied on a day-to-day basis. "It couldn't happen to me and, even if it does, we have all got to die sometime" is a common self-justification that almost belies belief when it is considered that a *life*-threatening "pleasure" is nothing more than a mere cigarette.

There may be some pleasures for which it is worth risking one's life but to do so for a cigarette is an illustration of the sheer insanity of addictive disease. Some habitual or excessive users can stop smoking when convinced by evidence of progressive respiratory and cardiovascular damage. Conversely, the sufferer from addictive disease cannot stop and denies the causal connection even up to his or her own death while blaming environmental pollution, an influenza epidemic, stress or any other external factor as the cause of his or her increasing disability.

The physical consequences (dizziness, headaches, tremor, increased pulse rate and blood pressure and increased urinary output leading to relative dehydration) of caffeine habituation (taking the equivalent of six or more cups of tea or coffee daily) – or addiction (the inability to stop using caffeine despite these adverse consequences) are not as well known as those of nicotine habituation or drug addiction but nonetheless can be very debilitating and the constant stimulant effect can lead to significant withdrawal symptoms, particularly causing headaches and chronic tiredness.

The physical effects of compulsive exercise can lead, for example, to sufferers continuing to exercise despite fractures or other serious consequences of their illness.

The social consequences of compulsive gambling and risk-taking, workaholism, compulsive overspending and other behavioural addictions can be utterly destructive.

The mental, emotional and other consequences are similar for all addictive disease.

The spiritual origin of all addictive disease is identical.

Where is the dividing line between normal use and addiction?

Typically where there are damaging consequences and where the sufferer feels the compulsion to continue to use or return to the substance or behaviour of addiction despite those damaging consequences.

Many damaging consequences can result from being a heavy drinker but alcoholism does not come simply from drinking too much. Alcoholism and other forms of addictive disease are more probably born rather than made. Similarly, there can be damaging consequences from repeated drug use, smoking, caffeine ingestion, gambling, excessive exercise, overwork, slimming, overeating, forced vomiting and from making inappropriate relationships but this does not mean that *all* people who suffer damaging consequences are necessarily addicted to any of these processes.

Three

Addictive use of any substance or behaviour is seen when the individual uses it inappropriately and compulsively to suppress uncomfortable emotions or to gain a sense of elation in order to change a disordered mood rather than simply using it for its own sake.

Are gambling and other forms of risk taking true addictions?

They can be. Risk-taking, including taking gambles of one kind or another, is part of normal life. As with other addictions, compulsive gambling and risk taking are seen when the sufferer is compelled to return despite repeated and increasing negative consequences and when the process is used inappropriately and compulsively to suppress uncomfortable emotions or to gain a sense of elation in order to change a disordered mood.

There is an element of risk-taking in all addictive disease and the "buzz" that is felt from a surge of adrenalin in risk-taking is similar to the "buzz" felt from addictive drugs. At the same time the adrenalin surge is itself a strong feeling and any strong feeling can be a trigger factor in stimulating the urge to use other mood-altering substances or processes. It is therefore advisable for people in recovery from any form of addictive disease that they should avoid gambling and other forms of risk-taking as far as possible.

The distress caused by compulsive gambling is very considerable. In those who do not have addictive disease, the occasional flutter on a horse race or on the football pools is comparable to the occasional pint of beer and therefore unlikely to be the cause of any major problems. But in the addictive disease of compulsive gambling the utter misery in the primary sufferer and in the family is every bit as devastating as in alcoholism.

It is easy to think of gambling as innocent pleasure. The Bingo of the housewife or pensioner certainly has its social value but if the relationship is addictive even this can become just as consuming as a Poker school or greyhound race. The consequences of compulsive gambling are comparable to those of any other addictive disease and are not simply those of financial loss. It may appear paradoxical but the compulsive gambler may get the biggest adrenalin surge from the biggest loss and, like the proverbial fisherman, may boast of the "one that got away".

Stealing (or not paying other debts) in order to gamble is commonplace and stories abound of any number of crimes - even murder - being committed for pitifully small amounts simply in order to gamble. This is addictive disease the same as any other and needs to be treated as such.

The coin-slot fruit machines of the amusement arcades may be joined nowadays by sophisticated video-games and the age of the gambler may progressively decrease but the addictive disease remains the same just as when the younger generation sometimes turns to solvents in place of the addictive use of alcohol or tranquillisers in their parents.

The financial markets are perhaps the biggest gamble of all and the dividing line between "normal" risk-taking and compulsive gambling, sharp practice and even criminality can become exceedingly thin. This is not to say that all investors or brokers are compulsive gamblers any more than to say that all drinkers are alcoholic. But it is to say that compulsive gambling with all its damaging consequences can be seen just as much in the reputable halls of commerce as in the street corner betting shop.

Gamblers Anonymous helps the primary spiritual disease.

How can relationships be addictive?

When an individual returns to making the same type of relationship again and again despite repeated and increasing negative consequences or, secondly, uses it inappropriately and compulsively to suppress uncomfortable emotions or, thirdly, to gain a sense of elation in order to change a disordered mood.

Some addictive relationships can be disguised as normal. Our society has tended to place women in a subservient relationship to men and some women find themselves drawn towards dominant or dependent partners and thus fail to assert their own needs as individuals. Either the dominance or the recession or both may be addictive in their repetitive pattern.

Other addictive relationships such as some sexual practices may be branded by society as being definitely abnormal or even criminal, yet there is evidence that they may be part of the broad spectrum of addictive disease and therefore outside the personal control of the individual sufferer. For example, there is evidence that child molestation runs in families and is not simply an individual quirk. There is a very high incidence of alcoholism in families where incest occurs but it also appears that child molestation occurs in several generations in some families even when there is no other obvious sign of addictive disease. This is not to argue that these practices should not be abhorred and punished by society but it is to say that the underlying tendency may be addictive in nature and may therefore require the specific treatment appropriate for any addictive disease.

Promiscuity may be used compulsively to suppress uncomfortable emotions or to gain a sense of elation in order to change a disordered mood and is a common cross-addiction with other forms of addictive disease.

Disordered relationships are the norm in any addictive disease and working on the capacity to make open and honest relationships is part of the recovery programme of any Anonymous Fellowship. For those not already helped in this way through other Anonymous Fellowships, Sex and Love Addicts Anonymous may provide the specific route to recovery.

It can reasonably be anticipated that whatever the addictive disease there will be an appropriate or near-appropriate Anonymous Fellowship. The strength of personal identification that an individual may receive from a particular Anonymous Fellowship will depend upon how much he or she has in common with the specific disease of the other sufferers. However, where there are small numbers of members of a particular Anonymous Fellowship it may be difficult to obtain sufficient numbers to get the maximum benefit from the group process. For example, Sex and Love Addicts Anonymous has only just begun in the UK whereas Alcoholics Anonymous has been in the UK for over forty years. There is therefore some potential disadvantage in trying to obtain maximum identification with other members of a particular Anonymous Fellowship and some advantage in recognising that all addictive disease - and all recovery programmes - have much that is fundamentally in common. Nonetheless the closest possible identification with other sufferer is preferable not only for each individual sufferer but also for the health of each Anonymous Fellowship.

Why do Chemical Dependency treatment centres tend not to emphasise the possible cross-addictive nature of nicotine, caffeine, sugar and white flour for people with addictive disease? Why do not all treatment centres specialising in eating disorders tend to emphasise the possible cross-addictive nature of alcohol, drugs, nicotine and caffeine?

Nicotine and caffeine are mood-altering but they are not obviously fully cross-addictive with alcohol and the various drugs that lead to Chemical Dependency or with sugar and white flour, the "drugs" of Eating Disorders. Therefore it does not seem to be necessary to encourage people who suffer from Chemical Dependency or Eating Disorders also to give up cigarette smoking (except on grounds of general health) for fear that it will spark off the compulsion to return to use of the original addictive drug of choice. Nonetheless, for spiritual recovery to have the best opportunity for development, it must be true that sufferers from any form of addictive disease would ultimately be best advised to avoid all substances and behaviours that may have an inappropriate mood-altering effect.

It has until now been the general policy within Chemical Dependency treatment centres specialising in addictive disease that nicotine, caffeine, sugar and white flour have generally been ignored – or their use may even be encouraged – in the early stages of treatment while sufferers learn to do without their prime drugs of choice in their recovery from Chemical Dependency. This policy is currently in question because of the high incidence of cross addiction to these substances but there is still a long way to go before Treatment Centres generally recommend abstinence from all these substances from the first day of recovery. The risk in doing so would be that new patients might well not see the need to do so and might feel that this would be an inappropriate intrusion into the realm of individual freedom of choice in their personal lives and, further, that life might not be much fun in the straitjacket of abstinence from all these substances as well as from their prime drugs of choice. The denial system is strong enough without giving the addictive disease any additional opportunity to manifest itself by giving the patient further excuse to leave treatment. These substances, that may in some people be of relatively minor cross-addictive potential, can always be tackled later when the head is more clear and the primary disease is in more secure recovery.

Treatment centres focus on first things first: alcohol and drugs may cause immediate threat to life itself in some sufferers, as can anorexia or bulimia or other forms of addiction in others. In each case the greatest threat needs to be addressed first and where two or more addictions are equally strong, then each needs to be treated with equal concern.

Are some forms of behaviour addictive?

Yes, any behaviour that is used inappropriately and compulsively to suppress uncomfortable emotions, or to gain a sense of elation in order to change a disordered mood, or to which someone repeatedly returns despite negative consequences, can be a form of addictive disease.

Compulsive taking of exercise is one example already mentioned. Some sufferers have been known to jog themselves literally to death, despite being told by doctors of the specific risks they would incur by taking further exercise.

Compulsive over-spending in these days of credit cards and generally easy credit facilities is not merely the privilege of the rich but can be a devastating condition in which inappropriate grandiosity repeatedly causes havoc with all efforts towards financial prudence.

Compulsive overworking (workaholism) or overachieving (which is not necessarily the same thing at all) are conditions that lead to much debate. The term "workaholic" may be used as a term of abuse but workaholism should not be confused with high energy and dedicated efforts towards a defined goal. Nonetheless, workaholism does exist when the sufferer simply cannot stop doing his or her work in order to suppress uncomfortable emotions or change a disordered mood and despite severe negative consequences to his or her family and to the rest of a balanced life. Similarly, overachieving can be an addiction if the achievement is to no purpose or gratification while at the same time the costs to other relationships may be so high as to be catastrophic.

Addictive behaviour is used just as addictive substances are used by people who are prone to addictive disease. It is used to suppress emotional feelings and it serves to isolate the sufferer from other people and to make him or her "special and different". To be special and different is excellent professionally when based upon talent and originality but on a personal level it is unjustifiable and hence a curse in human relationships.

What is the total number of people who have addictive disease?

Chemical Dependency appears to affect approximately 10% of the population. Some cultures, such as American Indians and the Irish, seem to have a particularly high incidence, while others, such as Jews, appear to have a particularly low incidence. The Italians appear less affected than the French. However, these estimations and cultural variations are difficult to verify, bearing in mind the wide variation in diagnostic criteria by differing individuals or schools of thought.

It is not known whether sufferers from the Eating Disorders and other addictive diseases have a separate addictive disease from Chemical Dependency or whether, as seems more probable, it is the same disease but with a different drug or activity of choice and with similar effects, consequences and recovery processes.

It is not known whether family members and others in close contact with sufferers from primary addictive disease are simply secondarily affected by the consequences of that addictive disease or whether some or all of them have addictive disease in their own right with their "drugs" of addiction being self-denial and caretaking for the primary sufferer himself or herself.

It may be that those family members who show signs of full addictive disease in their relationship with the primary sufferer are themselves primary sufferers from addictive disease. Thus, the truly addictive relationship may be seen when a primary sufferer uses a relationship as if it were a drug or when two primary sufferers are in a relationship together and one or other or both use that relationship as if it were a drug.

There is considerable overlap between the various groups of sufferers from one type of addiction and other groups. The children of those with addictive disease have a high chance of having it themselves. Eating disorders and other addictions are common in families in which there is Chemical Dependency. Eating disorders and Chemical Dependency not infrequently coexist in the same individual.

The intensity of particular cross-addictions will vary from one individual sufferer to another. Some will find one particular drug or behaviour of choice to be dominant but others may find several different addictions to be almost equally potent. Recovery from one specific addiction may lead to another gaining a stronger hold.

The total number of people who specifically have addictive disease is unknown and the total number of people whose lives are significantly affected by addictive disease of one kind or another in someone else is also unknown but it seems unlikely to be less than 25% of the total population. The numbers are unbelievable until we see them for ourselves.

What is the overall picture of the process of addictive disease?

Addictive disease originates as a disease of the human spirit. This predisposition may be genetically determined.

This leads to a disorder of mood.

Mood-altering substances or behaviours may be discovered by the individual sufferer specifically to alleviate the disorder of mood or to provide a sense of elation. The use of these specific substances or behaviours may trigger the underlying addictive potential so that they come to be used inappropriately and compulsively.

The intensity of addictive disease will vary from one individual to another.

All mood-altering substances or behaviours may be cross-addictive. Many individuals will have one particular "drug or behaviour of choice" and other substances or behaviours may be only mildly cross-addictive to them. Others will have more than one "drug or behaviour of choice" and may find themselves to be significantly cross-addicted to many others. In general, in any sufferer from addictive disease, recovery from addiction to one specific drug or behaviour may lead to activation of the addictive tendency towards another.

The continued addictive use of any substance or behaviour tends in time to lead to problems and to damaging consequences of use.

The causal connection between the addictive use and the damaging consequences may be denied.

The problems and damaging consequences of use will feed back to exacerbate further the underlying disorder of mood and this may lead to further use of addictive substances or behaviour. Thus, the addictive cycle progressively intensifies. (fig (v))

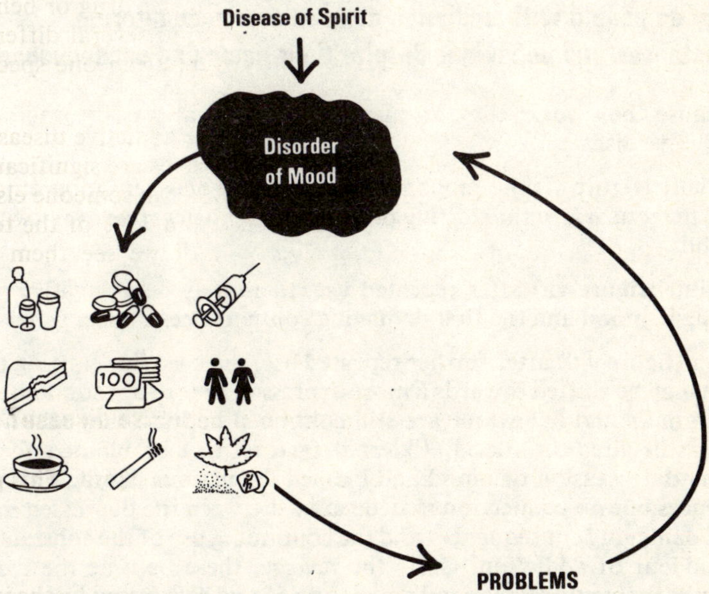

FIG (V)

4. Denial

Why do people with addictive disease use mood-altering substances and behaviour despite their damaging consequences?

Because they work: they *do* alter the mood that was disordered by addictive disease.

Initially (figure vi) the mood is improved, the new sensation enjoyed and the return is to the starting position, with no negative over-swing in mood.

In time (figure vii) after repeated use, there may be a negative over-swing in mood and the first damaging consequences of use.

Later (figure viii) after further repeated use, the base-line starting position may be shifted towards a more depressed state. The mood-altering substances and behaviour are still continued because they still work: they still alter the mood. External factors may be blamed for the general depression of mood and blamed for various damaging consequences but no connection may be made between the depressed mood and damaging consequences and the continuing use of the substance or behaviour of addiction. Quite the reverse, these become the trusted friends that truly understand and can be of real help in time of trouble. Any suggestion that they might be the *cause* of problems is simply denied: it is declared that they *could not* be.

Ultimately (figure ix) after even further repeated use, the base-line stating position is shifted so far towards a depressed state that even the trusted substances and behaviour of addiction cannot restore the mood to its original starting position from before they were ever used. Yet still they work in improving the mood from where it is now and still there may be no perception that the depressed mood and damaging consequences of use could possibly be the responsibility of the very substances and processes that seem to be the only things that can make life better. The causal connection between mood-altering substance or behaviour and the damaging consequences continues to be denied and the denial is intensified.

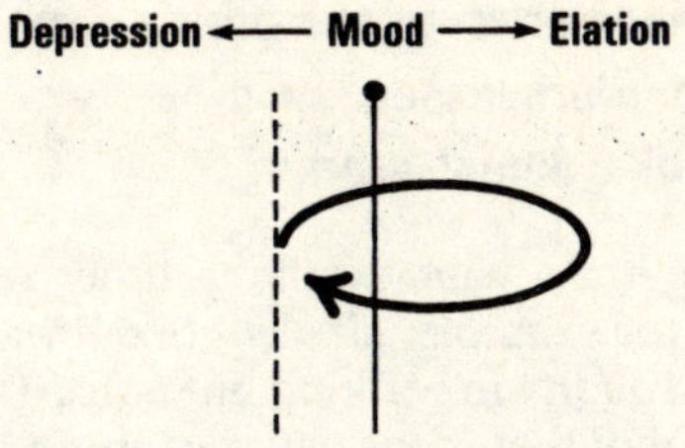

FIG (VI)

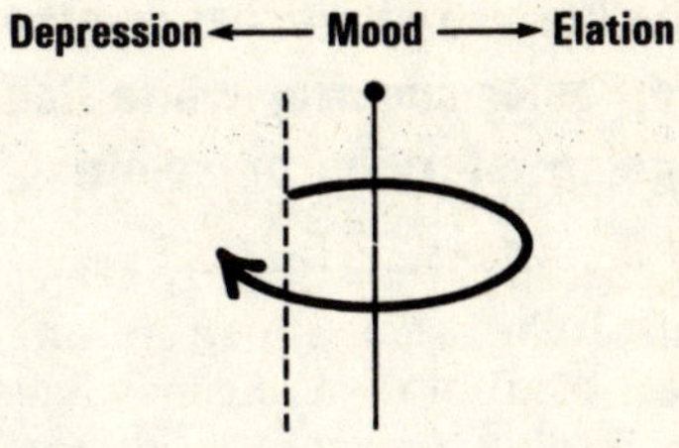

FIG (VII)

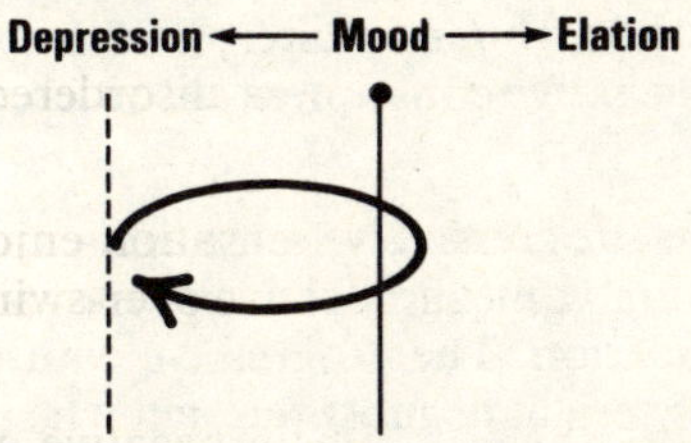

FIG (VIII)

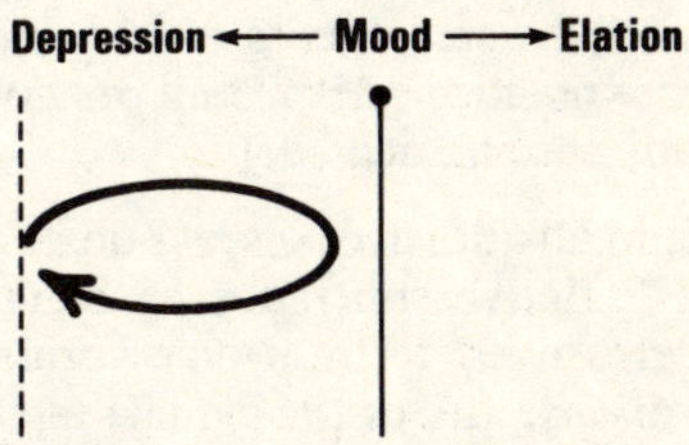

(FIG IX)

What is denial?

Denial is a psychological defence mechanism by which the sufferer simply does not believe that he or she has a problem, despite all the evidence.

Denial is found in any situation of acute stress and is, for example it is commonly seen in bereavement, redundancy, dismissal, divorce and in major disease or injury. The five progressive stages of any grieving process are:

i.	Denial	:	"It didn't happen".
ii.	Anger	:	"It shouldn't have happened to me"
iii.	Bargaining	:	"If I do this then maybe it won't hurt so much".
iv.	Depression	:	"My efforts are useless and there is nothing I can do".
v.	Acceptance	:	"Perhaps this is just the way it is and my life must go on".

The whole grief reaction often takes about two years to work through from initial denial to final acceptance.

Does the use of alcohol or other mood-altering substances, such as drugs or sugar or white flour, and processes, such as bingeing, starving or vomiting, make denial worse?

Yes, because they directly affect the brain which, among other functions, is the organ of perception. If, for example, all alcohol did was to affect the foot then one may have difficulty in walking but at least one may be able to perceive that it is alcohol that is the cause of those foot problems. But, as alcohol affects the brain itself, perception is impaired and the direct connection between alcohol consumption and various life problems is denied.

Yes, because giving up the substances or behaviour of addiction (the initially trusted agents of happiness through mood-alteration) triggers a grief reaction, despite all previous negative consequences (which may in any case be denied.)

Yes, in all addictive disease denial gets progressively worse as the use of the addictive substance or behaviours continue. The disease causes progressive deterioration of brain function. The progressive nature of the disease and of the denial system is seen at its most flagrant when the sufferer returns to use after many months or even years of abstinence. The descent to uncontrolled use is generally faster than previously and the "bottom of the pit", the level of degradation, the quantity of use and the severity of consequences are worse than ever before. Similar progressive deterioration in the disease and intensification of the denial system can be seen in all forms of addictive disease. It is as if the disease, with its associated denial system, progresses regardless of the intervening months or years of abstinence. There is therefore an unanswerable question on whether the use and the denial would have been even worse if they had been continuous rather than interrupted by abstinence.

Yes, but in the initial stages of the disease there are times of clarity between the fogs. In the morning before the first drink or in times of abstinence between binges or other epïsodes of addictive behaviour, there are opportunities for skilled, impartial, counsellors (particularly those who are themselves in recovery from addictive disease) to break through the denial system and thus intervene in the otherwise determined progression of the disease.

What are the features of denial in Eating Disorders?

i. Simple denial – the straightforward refusal to accept that something is so and that problems exist at all or have a direct connection with food intake or body weight or shape: "I can handle it".

ii. Minimising – accepting that there are problems but denying that they are of any great significance or that they necessarily have any connection with food intake or body weight or shape: "An anorexic, bulimic or overeater is someone who does more than I do".

iii. Externalisation or blaming – accepting that there are significant problems but blaming anything other than an eating disorder for their cause: "If it weren't for you I'd be okay".

iv. Rationalisation – accepting the problems, including the problems with food, but providing alibis: "Next time will be different".

v. Intellectualisation – accepting the problems and the specific food problems but getting heavily involved in analysis of intellectual theories or precise definitions of the various Eating Disorders and their causes and consequences: "Yes, but . . ."

vi. Diversion – changing the subject to focus upon anything other than food, body weight or shape or the consequences of Eating Disorders: "My real problem is . . ."

vii. Hostility – open attack at any mention of Eating Disorders and their consequences, let alone mention of the words "anorexia", "bulimia" or "overeating".

What are the features of denial in the other Addictive Diseases?

The various features of denial are exactly the same as for the Eating Disorders. Chemical Dependency, compulsive gambling or risk taking, addictive relationships and all other addictive diseases have the same pattern of denial as for the Eating Disorders. Simple substitution of the words "alcohol" or "drugs" or "risk-taking" or "behaviour" or whatever else is appropriate in place of the words "food" or "body weight or shape" will give a clear picture of the denial relevant to each particular addictive disease.

Denial spreads to cover cross-addictions. It is commonplace to find sufferers from alcoholism or drug addiction denying that they may themselves have food, nicotine or caffeine addictions or other compulsive behaviours and they may even deny that these other addictions are "real" addictions at all. They may prefer to believe themselves to be special and different in their primary addictions rather than part of a wider group of sufferers from addictive disease. The denial may persist and even be intensified when they are in recovery from their primary addiction. Similarly, sufferers from Eating Disorders may hotly deny that they have problems with alcohol or drugs or with shopping or spending or exercise.

What are the features of denial in Family Members?

i. Simple denial – refusal to see that there are any problems in the family.

ii. Minimising – acceptance that the sufferer has a problem and that there are some consequences in the family but refusal to accept that any of this is of great significance or that the family cannot cope from within its own resources.

iii. Externalisation or blaming – admitting that there are problems but saying that the causes are due to pressures at work or unemployment or due to social, financial or other stresses or due to doctors. Above all, family members frequently blame themselves – and they may be encouraged to do so by the primary sufferers.

iv. Rationalisation – admitting the problems but determinedly latching onto specific alternative reasons. "Depression" is a convenient port-manteau condition that frequently satisfies this purpose. "Bad company" is another. Considerable resistance may be encountered by anyone challenging these rationalisations.

v. Intellectualisation – interminable insistance upon precise definitions of terms and insistance upon pointing out minor differences rather than major similarities in the behaviour of the primary sufferers or family members when compared with others.

vi. Diversion – bringing up any number of reasons why the treatment of the individual sufferer, or consideration of the secondary effects upon the family, is not the prime problem requiring consideration at this particular time.

vii. Hostility – accusation that anyone mentioning Eating Disorders or having a different understanding of addictive disease from his or her own has a "bee in the bonnet".

Of course, any and all of these defences (particularly the last) may have an element of truth. But when one sees the whole lot in full flower all at once in one individual or in the whole family, one comes to accept the concept of denial as a prime component of "the family illness" in which the family member is addicted to self denial and caretaking for the primary sufferer and even (amazingly and hotly denied) addicted to the continuation of the status quo despite all its desperate features, just as the primary sufferer is addicted to the continuation of his or her own addictive behaviour despite its desperately damaging consequences.

What are the features of denial in the work-place?

i. Simple denial – refusal to accept that any staff have problems with Eating Disorders or other forms of addictive disease. This simple denial is not the same as refusing to accept that addictive disease is a management responsibility. That is a tenable argument as is the belief that in any case little that is practical can be done without help from outside agencies. Simple denial is when the problem is not seen in the first place, regardless of responsibility or resources.

ii. Minimising - admitting that one or two staff members are a bit fat or thin but insisting that the Company has more important problems to deal with and that it is not the Company rule nor responsibility to deal with these problems.

iii. Externalisation or blaming - The stresses and strains of a particular job or having too much money, or alternatively too little, may be blamed for Eating Disorders or other forms of addictive disease, despite the fact that these problems are widespread throughout the whole of society.

iv. Rationalisation - The social stigma of anorexia, bulimia or compulsive overeating is such that reasons for the Eating Disorder have to be found. Paradoxically, the disease concept (that Addiction of any kind is a disease that is not the fault of the sufferer) tends to be resisted by those who will happily accept "stress" or "depression" or "weak-will" or "upbringing" as possible causes. Similar rationalisations are found for any form of addictive disease.

v. Intellectualisation - Again, the fear that leads to interminable intellectualisation is understandable because of the social stigma of the Eating Disorders and addictive disease of any kind even though misdiagnosis has significant risks for the sufferer, for others in the work-place and for the Company itself.

vi. Diversion is seen firstly in discussion on the costs of treatment rather than the costs of continuing as before. Secondly, it is seen in a whole host of tactics and alternative strategies to the simple procedure of insisting that the sufferer goes for treatment just as he or she would do for any other disease.

vii. Hostility. The approach to the senior staff of a Company has to be very cautious when putting forward a policy for Eating Disorders or other forms of addictive disease in the work-place. It may be interpreted as a slur upon the good name of the Company and upon the management skills of the directors. They may well have been exasperated by the behaviour of someone in the work force who suffered from addictive disease and, understandably, may be even further exasperated by hearing the word "disease" used in this context. However well-intentioned, they simply may not know what to do for the best and this itself is a very irritating situation for them. Specifically as far as Eating Disorders are concerned, they may think it all very sad or peculiar but not really a Company problem. Sometimes individual staff members will have invested a great deal of time and effort into trying to help a sufferer from an Eating Disorder (especially someone with anorexia) and may be very wary of alternative suggestions for treatment.

What are the features of denial in the medical profession?

i. Simple denial – in five or six years of undergraduate training there is scant attention given to addictive disease of any kind. A negligible amount of time is spent on the primary condition of addictive disease that is associated with such a vast number of serious clinical consequences. Undergraduates and qualified doctors alike spend considerably more time on consequences rather than on the cause or nature of addiction and may consider the latter to be none of their business.

ii. Minimising – Frequently even the partners of a large group medical practice are not aware of any addiction problems or Eating Disorders among patients on their combined lists of patients – except for one or two "pitiful anorexics or hopeless obese cases for whom it would be cruel to do anything". The treatment centre reports on some of their patients must come as a complete surprise!

iii. Externalisation and blaming – Political circumstances may be blamed for the inability of doctors to do much for sufferers from Eating Disorders or other forms of addictive disease. There may be some truth in this but it is questionable whether doctors in general would be keen to expand this particular aspect of their work even if they had all the resources they could wish for. Further, doctors, as much as any other group of people, tend to blame the patient for the primary condition of any addiction or Eating Disorder.

iv. Rationalisation – every doctor has his or her own theories on the causes of Eating Disorders and all other forms of addictive disease and a monotonous range of fervent beliefs, coupled with negligible clinical experience, somehow finds its way into the medical press.

v. Intellectualisation – The disease concept still tends to be fiercely resisted by some members of the medical profession on the grounds that Eating Disorders and addictions are self-inflicted conditions and are not "real" diseases.

vi. Diversion – The pressure upon a doctor's time is the standard, readily available myth for all such challenges.

vii. Hostility – Cases abound where General Practitioners remove patients suffering from Chemical Dependency from their lists of registered patients. Hospitals often get rid of Alcoholic or drug addicted patients (the same patients time and time again) as soon as they are medically "safe". Similar hostility may be shown towards sufferers from other forms of addictive disease. Recent attitude surveys showed that doctors were *less* likely to want to care for patients suffering from addictive disease after being exhorted to do so by the Government. In the case of Eating Disorders, doctors may get angry with compulsive overeaters who say that the "cannot" stop eating. Alternatively they may get angry with everyone else other than the sufferer from anorexia when they desperately try to help in their own way. The sufferer from bulimia is commonly not even recognised because everything seems all right on the outside.

What are the features of denial in society at large?

i. Simple denial – We see the tramps and drop-outs and may wrongly assume that they are necessarily addicted to alcohol or drugs. The Eating Disorders and other forms of addictive disease may not be seen at all except in their extreme forms. We see fatties and thinnies and it rarely occurs to us that they might be unable to control their condition. We do not see that our own friends and colleagues have the same one in ten incidence of addictive disease as anyone else's friends or colleagues.

ii. Minimising – "Our area may have a problem but I''ve never seen it except for the pushers hanging about that dreadful housing estate". Meanwhile, the hordes beating a path to the pub or the off-licence are simply ignored and sympathy is given to those who take copious amounts of prescription drugs for their "nerves" or for "insomnia". Slimming diets or health farms and various horrendous surgical procedures are seen as the standard appropriate solution for compulsive overeaters, while sufferers from anorexia or bulimia are deemed to require psychotherapy or, better still, a stiff talking to.

iii. Externalisation or blaming – "the Government ought to do something" is the almost universal cry, but precisely what it ought to do varies with the beliefs and prejudices of the individual. The "drug barons", importing from Thailand, Pakistan, or Colombia, are seen as the real cause of increasing "hard" drug addiction in the UK, rather than the fact that they would have no market if there were no demand. The failure of the National Health Service is inappropriately blamed for the failure of standard psychiatric treatment for Eating Disorders.

iv. Rationalisation – we all of us find plenty of reasons – parties, suppers, weddings and celebrations of any kind – for drinking or overeating. We put our own reasons onto those who are addicted to alcohol or food in order to explain why they drink or eat so much; "he's a good chap, enjoying himself, having a bit of fun, relaxing, celebrating . . . but on occasions he goes a bit over the top". Similar rationalisations are used to "explain" the behaviour of sufferers from the other eating disorders and other forms of addictive disease.

v. Intellectualisation – the press and television are daily crammed with the opinions of the pundits. There are perhaps two things upon which each of us is the indisputable world expert, firstly the function of our own bowels and hence those of everyone else and secondly the causes of and treatment for Eating Disorders and addiction of any kind.

vi. Diversion – showing that one does have some practical experience of treating Eating Disorders and other forms of addiction can be guaranteed to result in a change in the topic of conversation.

vii. Hostility – "I suppose you think that we're all alcoholics or addicts of some kind and that we all ought to give up everything we enjoy". Such anger and defensiveness is commonplace and understandable because our society is accustomed to the stereotype pictures of alcoholism and drug addiction and Eating Disorders as conditions of weak-willed or immoral people who need to be taught firm lessons on how to behave themselves properly rather than as ill people who need to be helped to become well.

CHAPTER **Five**

5. The Family Disease

What is the Family Disease?

Partly it is the response of some family members to the addictive disease of the primary sufferer.

Partly it is a primary addictive disease of some family members who are addicted to "fixing" or "helping" other people regardless of the consequences to themselves or to those other people whom they seek to help.

Do all members of the family necessarily have the family disease?

Not necessarily – or, if they do, it appears to affect some considerably less than others.

Isn't it perfectly reasonable to react to having addictive disease in the family?

Yes it is. A family member who did not react to the craziness of Eating Disorders or other addictive disease would be a very strange, unreactive, person who might well be considered to be at least odd if not ill or crazy himself or herself for not reacting.

What are the normal reactions to addictive disease in any family?

Anxiety for the primary sufferer and for other members of the family.

Disgust at the actions of the primary sufferer and at the consequences of the disease.

A sense of inadequacy and frustration because one may not understand what one is observing nor know what on Earth one can do about it.

Fear for the future.

Anger with the primary sufferer, with one's self and with other members of the family and with anyone else who happens to be around.

Shame that such a thing could happen in one's own family.

Guilt that the family member himself or herself may possibly have been in part a cause of the problem in the primary sufferer either by something done or not done.

Blaming the primary sufferer, other members of the family and all those who are considered to have contributed to the problem.

Initial disbelief in the disease concept and determination to find or re-inforce one's own ideas on the cause of addiction.

Determination to deal with the situation "properly and once and for all" but coupled with confusion of not knowing precisely what to do for the best, particularly in the face of vast quantities of advice all of which seems perfectly clear – except that it directly conflicts with other equally vast and equally clear advice from other sources.

Love and concern for the primary sufferer and for other members of the family.

A sense of loss of mutually supportive family relationships.

The standard grief reaction going through the five phases of denial, anger, bargaining, depression and finally acceptance over a period of two years but sometimes with progressive insulation of emotions resulting in a sense of isolation.

What are the indications of addictive family disease?

Exactly the same as for the primary addictive disease of any of the Eating Disorders or any other form of addictive disease. The object of the family addiction (or the "drug") is self denial and caretaking for the primary sufferer himself or herself. Thus, the addictive family disease is addiction to people who have primary addictive disease.

The family member is determined to "help" the primary sufferer:

(a) regardless of whether this "helping" actually does help in the long term. The family member will continue to do things for the primary sufferer (providing food and shelter and other necessities of life, tidying up the messes, telling lies or half-truths to "cover up", paying off debts or fines, providing bail, apologising on his or her behalf and generally doing everything possible to protect the primary sufferer from the consequences of his or her disease) regardless of the demonstrable fact that these actions do *not* help the sufferer to get into recovery. The family member will say that these things *should* help, that they are only part of normal family commitment and civilised behaviour and that, if family members did not do these things, then the primary sufferer might die. The sad truth is that the primary sufferer is much more likely to die if this "enabling" support continues. All help is simply converted by the primary sufferer into more opportunity to continue the addiction. The heartfelt promises of the morning are frequently broken by nightfall. The choice is not between life and death but between possible death and probable death.

(b) regardless of the price that the family member is paying in his or her own life. Again the family member will argue that this is perfectly reasonable behaviour for any family: total commitment regardless of cost to self might be considered to be the moral basis of family life. That might be so in the case of other illness or disaster but in addictive disease total commitment regardless of cost to self actually works against recovery. Not only is there failure to confront the primary sufferer with the full consequences of addictive disease but also there is no significant contrast between the general behaviour and quality of life in the primary sufferer and in the family member. Why should the primary sufferer want to seek recovery if the quality of life without an Eating Disorder, or other addictive disease, is going to be no better than that of the family member? The primary sufferer continues his or her addiction regardless of consequences and so does the family member: the addictive disease is similar; only the object of the addiction differs.

Addictive disease is primary (not secondary to other conditions), progressive and relapsing. The primary sufferer progressively adapts to the changes brought about by the disease. The family member also progressively adapts so that the effects of the disease are largely the progressive effects of that adaptation. The disease always gets worse if it is not treated but nonetheless the family member develops ways in which he or she can somehow live with the disease. Family routines are adjusted to accommodate the worsening disease. The family member tends to react to crises brought about by the addictive disease as if addiction were just like any other acute disease. Thus, he or she will tend to resolve the crisis rather than use it as a lever towards treatment.

The family members may come to blame external factors or blame each other for the addictive disease of the primary sufferer. They fail to control his or her use of the substance or process of addiction so, next, they may attempt to control what they perceive as his or her "reasons" for use and come to protect him or her from its consequences. They fail also in this.

What are the characteristics of addictive family disease?

Similar to those of the primary disease.

Preoccupation: The family member's life is haunted day and night by thoughts on what might be happening to the primary sufferer and what action might or might not be taken to help. The family member is faced constantly with one dilemma after another.

Use alone: The family member becomes progressively isolated from friends and from all social contact as the process of "helping" becomes more absorbing.

Use for effect: The family member avoids facing up to other problems by focussing attention on the problem of the primary sufferer's addictive disease.

Use as a medicine: The repeated episodes of anxiety stimulate secretion of adrenalin and this may be used subconsciously as a stimulant. As with all stimulants, depression sets in when the initial stimulant effect wears off and a further dose of stimulant is required to counteract the depression.

Protecting supply: It is absolutely extraordinary to note how some family members will appear to do almost everything in their power to *prevent* the primary sufferer getting into recovery. Not uncommonly, family members will pour scorn on the philosophy of Alcoholics Anonymous and related Fellowships for Eating Disorders even though (and perhaps even because) the programme works, whereas the family member's methods of treatment – time and time again – have failed to help the primary sufferer. Pride may be hurt.

On some occasions family members will attempt to sabotage treatment saying that the primary sufferer is being brainwashed, ought to be at home, ought to learn to behave like everybody else and ought to do all manner of things that have failed before and will fail again to help addictive disease. On rare occasions family members have even been known to take alcohol or drugs or "special" foods into treatment centres "to lessen the suffering" or "because we were asked". By protecting the supply of alcohol or drugs or particular foods for the primary sufferer, the family member protects his or her own supply of self-denying and caretaking.

Using more than planned: Time and again the family member gives more time and money and other forms of support to the primary sufferer than he or she can afford or than was intended.

Higher capacity than others: The capacity of family members to absorb punishment and come up asking for more is simply phenomenal.

Any doubt there may be that the family disease is a genuine addictive disease is dispelled when the divorced wife of a primary sufferer promptly marries another or when the parents of young sufferers find themselves depressed and lonely and wondering what to do with their time and experience once their own primary sufferer is in recovery.

What are the consequences of the family disease?

Again, similar to those of the primary illness.

Spiritual: Damage to trust, hope, faith and love.

Emotional: Mood swings. Recurrent anxiety and depression with progressive deterioration.

Behavioural: Changes in values so that other people's behaviour that would previously not have been accepted becomes progressively more tolerated if it relates to an Eating Disorder or other form of addictive disease.

Social: Progressive isolation from previous friends and social contacts.

Legal: Family members may get themselves into legal difficulties by "covering-up" for the actions of primary sufferers.

Marital: Many a parental marriage is broken by the amount of focus put on the problems of the child primary sufferer rather than upon improving the marital relationship and giving each other support in the time of crisis. In the situation where the family member is married to the primary sufferer, the family member may tolerate progressive destruction of all that he or she should reasonably expect from married life. Instead of early insistence that no further deterioration in the relationship will be tolerated, the family member may even collude with further decline and adopt a negative posture of blameless martyr.

Professional: The family member may give progressively less attention to his or her own work because of the problems at home and may even change employment in order to have more time or opportunity to supervise the worsening chaos at home.

Intellectual: Mental work requires a calm mind which is precisely what family members believe (understandably but wrongly) cannot be acquired while there is active addictive disease in the family.

Educational: The family member's own opportunities for further education become reduced almost to zero.

Financial: Paying for the consequences of the addictive disease of the primary sufferer can be exceedingly expensive and families may even be much more willing to pay for almost anything than to pay towards the costs of treatment in a specialist addiction unit. The perceived disgrace and deprivation of in-patient treatment are likened to a prison sentence and are commonly felt to be consequences that are best avoided whereas they may in fact be the crucial turning point that bring the primary sufferer and the family member into full realisation of the seriousness of addictive disease and the need to seek continuing recovery.

Physical: The deterioration of physical health in family members becomes obvious for all to see – as obvious as that of the primary sufferer.

What are the personality traits of the family disease?

Again, they correspond to those of the primary disease.

Conflict With Authority: Family members may repeatedly try to cover up for the misdeeds or mishaps of the primary sufferer and may be exceedingly angry with various domestic or civil "authorities" when they themselves are found out. They claim, as do the primary sufferers, that the authorities "do not understand".

Criticism of others: Understandable bitterness and envy of the apparently normal lives of other people frequently result in generalised criticism in all directions.

Intellectualisation: The family members usually have clearer heads than the primary sufferers and use them for even more determined discussion of "facts" rather than facing up to and discussing the emotional pain of their own position.

Anger and Resentment: Again these are felt to be justified but they are spiritual poisons nonetheless and they destroy the emotional life of the family member.

Stubbornness: The resistance to change in ideas on addictive disease tends to be considerably beyond what is required for normal intellectual scepticism.

Self-Centredness: Eating Disorders may become the centre of all conversation and activity to the neglect of social needs and the needs of other, non-addicted, members of the family.

Pride: Pride causes much wilful action in pursuit of solutions to the problems of Eating Disorders and any form of addictive disease. The determination to find a personal, individual, solution is characteristic of being a "caretaker" or "fixer" which is itself the hallmark of the family disease.

Procrastination: Everything else other than the problems of addictive disease is put aside "for the time being".

Self-pity: Having addictive disease in the family is a lonely situation but it is made more so by the spiritual isolation. Self-pity tends to block taking action that will be truly effective in reversing the downward spirals of primary and family diseases.

Perfectionism: Family members try desperately to get everything exactly right in their plans for the primary sufferer but still blame themselves when the smallest thing goes wrong.

Externalisation: Family members, like the primary sufferers, blame all manner of people, places and things for the problems caused by primary addictive disease but have little insight into their own condition.

Denial: As with the primary illness, family members cannot see their own addictive disease and may be exceedingly indignant if it is pointed out to them. In time, through an appropriate Family Fellowship (for each primary addictive disease there is an Anonymous Fellowship and also a corresponding Family Fellowship, for example O-Anon corresponds to Overeaters Anonymous, Al Anon corresponds to Alcoholics Anonymous and Families Anonymous to Narcotics Anonymous) the sufferers from the family disease learn to see their own disease and recovery mirrored in the other members of that Anonymous Fellowship. If there is no family Fellowship corresponding to the appropriate primary Anonymous Fellowship in a particular geographical area then attendance at meetings of Al Anon or Families Anonymous are helpful by providing the nearest equivalent programme for recovery for family members.

How do you know if you have "Family Disease"

You probably do not - because of denial - but it would be helpful initially to do the following self-assessment or go through it with a counsellor specialising in addictive disease:

PROMIS Recovery Centre. Step I for families

The "drugs" of addictive "family disease" are self-denial of one's own feelings and needs and addictive caretaking for the feelings and needs of others. In order to help family members see past their own "denial system", for the purposes of this assessment, "addiction" means any form of repetitive or apparently compulsive behaviour, "addict" refers to the person involved and "drug" refers to the substance or behaviour of his or her choice.

A. *Self-denial.*

1. Write down examples of when you last:

- **i.** went to the cinema or theatre or a sporting event
- **ii.** had some friends round for the evening
- **iii.** had a holiday away from home
- **iv.** played a game of some kind
- **v.** read a book for fun

2. How much time would you spend on these preceding five things in an average week, month or year?

3. Write down examples of when you last

- **i.** read an article on addiction
- **ii.** cancelled a social engagement or abandoned plans for something pleasurable.
- **iii.** stayed up late at night talking to someone who is under the influence of drugs.
- **iv.** stayed away from work or from some important personal activity in order to do something "necessary" for the addict in your life.
- **v.** gave money or goods or services to the addict in your life when you could not really afford to part with these things.

4. How often have you done these preceding five things in an average week or month or year?

5. Write down further examples of where you yourself are aware of episodes of self-denial in order to help the addict in your life.

B. Caretaking.

1. Write down examples of when you last:

- **i.** provided food, clothing or other "necessities" for the addict in your life because he or she could not afford them.
- **ii.** gave money to the addict in your life because he or she would be in trouble if you did not.
- **iii.** provided accommodation to the addict in your life because he or she had nowhere else to go.
- **iv.** told a lie to someone else in order to protect the addict in your life from getting into even worse trouble.
- **v.** took personal or financial responsibility for something that had been done by the addict in your life.

2. How often have you done these things in an average week or month or year?

3. Write down examples of when you last:

   i. took on extra work in order to provide something for the addict in your life.

   ii. tidied up a significant physical mess left behind by the addict in your life.

   iii. tried to soothe down a damaged personal relationship of the addict in your life.

   iv. tried to protect a professional or educational relationship of the addict in your life.

   v. paid off debts or fines or loans of the addict in your life.

4. How often have you done these things in the last week, month or year?

5. Write down further examples of where you yourself are aware of episodes of caretaking for the addict in your life in order to diminish the damaging consequences of his or her addictive disease and where you have given "just one more chance" for him or her to get straight.

C. *Powerlessness.*

1. Write down examples of previous relationships that have followed similar patterns to the one that you now have with the addict in your life.

D. *Unmanageability.*

1. Write down examples of where in any of your present or previous relationships you have found your own life has become significantly and progressively more chaotic and damaged.

What happens to children brought up in families in which there is an Eating Disorder or addictive disease of any kind?

These families are referred to as "dysfunctional" which means that they do not function in the "normal" manner of other families. They have no idea what "normal" is and therefore they invent it for themselves and may be very wide of the mark that other families set for themselves. Television "soap opera" families may be so "perfect" as to be distinctly abnormal.

There are various stereotype behavioural patterns that children in these families tend to adopt when one or other or both parents have some form of primary addictive disease. These are only stereotypes and each child in a family may have some characteristics of several of these behavioural patterns rather than fit one particular stereotype.

i.	Hero	: This child believes that he or she can only obtain love and appreciation through achievement.
ii.	Delinquent or scape-goat	: This child gets his or her status from identification with similar "delinquent" children in other families.
iii.	Caretaker or "lost" child	: This child takes responsibility for the family and looks after it by gently blending into the background and keeping the peace.
iv.	Comedian or mascot	: This child, often the youngest of the family, is treated as a pet and is not meant to be bothered by "serious" matters.

In each case these children do not have any clear picture of reality and they are not able to express or receive full gratification for their own needs.

Whatever their personality type, these children have a significant risk of primary addictive disease and they will also tend to marry people with primary addictive disease.

As they grow into adult life they find that many of the conflicts and confusions of childhood are unresolved. They have difficulty in feeling or expressing their own emotions and in making successful relationships. Help for this is available through the Anonymous Fellowship of Adult Children of Alcoholics, which aims to assist the grown-up children of any addictive family.

What is the treatment for the family disease?

Similar to that for continuing care for the primary addictive disease.

i. Attend regular meetings of the appropriate Anonymous Fellowship for family members and get an individual "sponsor" from the Fellowship.

ii. Read regularly the approved literature of that Fellowship.

iii. Work the twelve steps for recovery suggested by that Fellowship.

Is this treatment brain-washing?

Yes, in a way it is, it helps to clear the mind of all sorts of rubbish and to focus attention on improving the family member's own life. This is done for its own sake but it is found that the primary sufferer will quite commonly seek treatment through his or her appropriate Anonymous Fellowship within a few months of the family member seeking his or her own recovery. However, it should be emphasised that the Family Fellowships exist for the benefit of the family member, regardless of what may be happening to the primary sufferer.

The Anonymous Fellowships do not give specific advice for individual problems. Each member is free to decide whatever action is appropriate within the general guidelines of the twelve steps and twelve traditions of the Fellowship.

No dues or fees are required by the Family Fellowships, especially not from newcomers. No donations are sought or accepted from outside sources and even gifts and legacies from members are restricted financially.

The God or Higher Power of the Anonymous Fellowships is strictly a personal, private choice and there is no religious affiliation. Atheists, in religious terms, can and do follow the programme.

Anonymity guarantees that confidences are respected and there is no possible personal follow-up except at meetings at which attendance is obviously voluntary in any case.

Is treatment for the family disease necessary at all?

Only if the family member finds it helpful.

The experience of the Anonymous Fellowships, and of Treatment Centres based upon their principles, is that the sufferers from primary addictive disease have a better chance of sustained recovery if the close family members attend corresponding appropriate Family Fellowships.

Treatment centres usually have family programmes, some of which are residential.

Family members attending appropriate Family Fellowships often find that the quality of their own lives improves significantly even if the primary sufferer is not in recovery.

Psychotherapy, Family Therapy, religious teaching and various other forms of "therapy" are not found to be significantly helpful in the treatment of primary addictive disease nor in addictive family disease, although they may provide supplementary help to some individuals after they are in recovery through the Anonymous Fellowships.

What is tough love?

The capacity to love the individual sufferer while confronting the disease and making the sufferer fully responsible for the consequences of all his or her actions.

"Tough love" should have equal emphasis on both words and the toughness applies as much to the family member as to the primary sufferer.

The tough love hurts the family member not simply because it involves allowing the pimary sufferer to experience the full painful consequences of the Eating Disorder or other form of addictive disease but also because it involves the family member in resisting his or her own addictive urges to "fix" all the problems and manage the life of the primary sufferer.

Tough love should be kind, gentle and understanding to both the family member and the primary sufferer, while nonetheless allowing each to be fully responsible for his or her own feelings and behaviour and for taking the full consequences of all choices of individual action.

Sometimes a family member will believe that tough love involves refusal to help the sufferer to seek recovery, for example by refusing to pay for specific 12 Step Programme counselling or in-patient treatment. This is simply "black-belt Al Anon" behaviour: hoping to repay the primary sufferer for all the pain felt by the family member.

Further, a family member may find it difficult to "let go" of the primary sufferer while he or she is in treatment and may still want to find out everything that goes on in a Treatment Centre on a day-to-day basis and thereby continue to "fix" by proxy. Tough love requires that the family member "lets go" of the primary sufferer and seeks help for himself or herself from the appropriate Family Fellowship, concentrating primarily on his or her *own* recovery from the addictive urge to fix or control the lives of others.

This tough love in the family member is, more than anything else, what tends to bring the primary sufferers to seek their own recovery. But, even then, it may fail and it should again be emphasised that family members benefit for their *own* sake from involvement in the Family Fellowships regardless of what may happen to the primary sufferer.

Precisely what is involved in tough love in allowing the sufferer from addictive disease to take the full consequences of his or her disease?

In eating disorders:

not involving yourself at all in anything whatever to do with how or when or how much the primary sufferer eats or does not eat.

not allowing the primary sufferer to be inappropriately involved in food preparation.

not allowing any form of inappropriate behaviour.

not providing special foods or special portions.

In alcoholism:

not clearing up physical messes caused by the primary sufferer.

not apologising to other people for the behaviour of the primary sufferer.

not telling lies to the employer, the courts or anyone else.

not paying off the debts of the primary sufferer.

not putting up bail or hiring lawyers to defend in any alcohol-related case.

not allowing yourself or your children to be passengers in a car if the driver is the primary sufferer and he or she has been drinking.

not altering your own social life and neglecting your own friendships.

not taking on more work yourself in order to take over financial responsibility from the primary sufferer while he or she continues to drink.

not going along with stories of depression or stress.

not allowing children to suffer in any way: if one parent is the primary sufferer the inter-parental relationship can possibly be restored *after* the primary sufferer is in recovery.

not doubting your own sanity or believing that the problems are all your fault.

In drug addiction:

not allowing any illegal drugs in your own home: threaten to call the police if you do find drugs or have serious reason to suspect their use. All threats *must* be carried out. Give no second chances and accept no "explanations".

in adults and in children old enough to be independent, offer a straight choice: drugs or home – and stick to it.

not paying fines, putting up bail or finding lawyers for any drug-related offences.

not providing money to pay debts or even to buy "essentials". Any money given will either be spent directly on drugs or, alternatively, gifts in kind will either be sold or will enable other money to be spent on drugs.

not obtaining addictive drugs or collecting prescriptions on behalf of the sufferer.

reporting all thefts to the Police.

In compulsive behaviour of any kind:

not taking responsibility yourself for any consequences of the behaviour of the primary sufferer.

not easing the burden of the consequences in any way.

not failing to look after your own needs.

In the Family disease:

not allowing the family member to take any form of responsibility that should rightly belong to the primary sufferer or to someone else.

not being taken in by the belief that "help" of one kind or another really is helpful: it may actually hinder someone else's growth towards maturity.

What can family members and others do to help someone who has an Eating Disorder or some other form of addictive disease?

Recognise that he or she (whether suffering from the primary disease or the family disease) is in the grip of a disease that controls much of his or her words and actions. Occasionally there will still be glimpses of the real person, pleading for help and desperately trying to be free. But then the alien disease, like a persistent parasite, takes hold again and for a time destroys everything in its path: all hope, all trust, all honesty, all love, all relationships. And then again comes a glimpse of the suffering individual: confused, frightened and lonely. And then the disease smashes in yet again, utterly arrogant in its demand for total control, determined to have all the answers in any discussion, determined to make everyone else feel helpless, frustrated, angry and isolated and determined to use the words and actions of the sufferer to its own absolute advantage.

Avoid trying to reason with the disease. Stay quietly confident of your own knowledge of truth. Seek the help of O-Anon, Al Anon or Families Anonymous or other appropriate Anonymous Family Groups in order to meet other people who have similar first-hand experience of the living hell of being at close quarters with the insanity of addictive disease. Learn from them to love the sufferer while still hating his or her disease. Learn from them the strength to risk to say no to the disease: to refuse to cover up, tidy up or pay up but allow the sufferer to take the full consequences of the addiction. Be assured that the risks taken now would later on be even greater as the disease progresses. Learn from the Family Fellowships to allow your own sanity to redevelop by letting go of the self-imposed stranglehold of trying to be a "caretaker" for someone else.

Recognise that alcohol, cannabis, cocaine, LSD, heroin, Methadone, minor tranquillisers, sleeping tablets and many other mood-altering substances may all be cross-addictive to sufferers from any form of addictive disease and that all these drugs may feed the disease regardless of whether they are legal, illegal or medicinally prescribed.

Recognise that there is no blame in Eating Disorders or any form of addiction. As with short sight, diabetes, epilepsy and many other diseases or conditions, it happens in some people but not in others. Addictive disease, as opposed to physiological addiction, is probably not a significant potential risk for *all* human beings.

Recognise that addictive disease affects different people in different ways and is very variable in its intensity but that all share the denial of believing that they are not addicted: the crucial test of addiction is not whether one can stop the use of an addictive substance or behaviour but whether one can happily stay off and not be drawn back to it or to something equally addictive.

Recognise that although Eating Disorders and other forms of addictive disease, like short sight, are probably genetically inherited and certainly run in families, this does not mean that all parents or all children of sufferers from any form of addictive disease will necessarily have addictive disease themselves. It helps the sufferer to know that while you hold him or her accountable for all actions, you do not hold him or her responsible for having addictive disease in the first place.

Learn to *be* things rather than *do* things for the sufferer. A true friend would not do anything that would enable the disease to continue but would instead take the difficult and risky path of totally confronting it, while still loving the sufferer, despite all the harshness that the disease will cause the sufferer to throw in return. The risk of confronting the disease may be the possible death of the sufferer; the risk of not doing so may be his or her almost certain death from the progression of the disease.

Recognise in time, perhaps only from the despair of repeated failure, that family members did not *cause* the disease, cannot control it and cannot cure it and that in time they may need to surrender the fight and hand over the care of the sufferer's addictive disease to his or her own appropriate Anonymous Fellowship. In due course in recovery the primary sufferer and the family member can be reunited in a happier and more fulfilling relationship than ever before.

Interlude

Addictive disease has common characteristic features that are shared by many if not all sufferers. Some of the features of alcoholism in its terminal phase are so well known that a cartoonist has only to draw a couple of lines for everyone to know that the subject is a "drunk". Similarly, many other forms of compulsive behaviour are easily recognised even though there may be considerable debate if one has the temerity to apply the term "addiction".

Early diagnosis is difficult partly because the denial systems of primary sufferers, family members and others make it hard to get a clear picture, especially when there may be few adverse consequences. Cross-addictions may be hotly denied because the subject matter may for some be too close for comfort. Sometimes in truth they do not exist: not all human behaviour is addictive in nature and one has to keep a sense of balance.

The compulsive overeater may be mocked while the sufferer from anorexia may be pitied, the compulsive gambler scorned, the drug addict feared and the family member treated with half concern and half criticism. These are simply the reactions of a fearful public, generally uninformed on the nature of addictive disease and unable to distinguish between the disease and the sufferer.

Yet all this is easily understood in comparison to grasping the concepts of recovery. The progressive decline in the course of addictive disease follows similar patterns in differing individual sufferers. But each person's recovery is unpredictable. The analogy with short sight, so useful in considering the nature of the disease, is not nearly so helpful in considering recovery. Certainly there are daily actions that help someone to stay in recovery just as the daily wearing of spectacles or contact lenses helps to overcome the effects of short sight. But there the analysis ends: there is no clear parallel to the apparent inability of some sufferers to get into substantial recovery, if at all, and there is nothing to correspond to the process of relapse even when, on the face of it, all recommendations are being followed.

The plain fact is that one may learn something about the general features of recovery by looking at large numbers of individuals but the converse does not wholly follow. The generalisations are no more than that.

Nonetheless there are some general patterns that may be helpfully described even though any individual sufferer may rightly say that the entire pattern does not apply to him or her. It is of course also true that no individual's disease is exactly like that of another. But the individual variations in the patterns of disease are less wildly unpredictable than those of recovery.

Indeed it has been postulated that the true process of recovery dates from when the sufferer first recognises that perhaps all is not in perfect control. This recognition can pre-date the actual cessation of the substance or behaviour of addiction by some considerable time. The continuing use after that recognition is a time of testing whether control is possible or whether it has indeed been lost. Consequently, the boundary between what the sufferer considers to be "normal" or "addictive" is repeatedly pushed further away. During this time of testing, a sufferer from an Eating Disorder may say that the problem is simply a matter of diet or shape or clothing or personal preference in various aspects of life. Similarly, a sufferer from alcoholism may say that he or she cannot be alcoholic because he or she does not drink in the mornings or is still in regular employment or still has a home and family or perhaps only drinks wine and beer but never spirits or that he or she only drinks at weekends. All these may be no more than attempts at testing control while there may be an underlying awareness that all is not well.

But, as the disease progresses, the boundary between "normal" and "addictive" recedes beyond the level where other people are convinced about the normality of the sufferer. There may be justifications such as "stress" or "depression" and indeed these factors do feature very significantly in the lives of sufferers from any form of addictive disease but they are consequences and not causes.

Ultimately, only the strength of the denial system enables the sufferer to function at all. Self worth diminishes and shame and fear increase as the disease progresses. The progression of destruction moves from affecting spiritual values to affecting the capacity for a full range of emotional feelings and then into affecting intellectual processes and finally affecting physical health, although there will of course have been many episodes of some damage to physical well-being throughout the progress of the disease. The mirror of self-perception becomes progressively more distorted and inaccurate. Relationships with self, with others and with God – or with spiritual values in life – become increasingly strained and impaired. This is the nature and progression of addictive disease. This is the picture of the pathetic mess of a human being who ultimately, in desperation, seeks recovery.

The process of recovery involves the gradual reversal of all these processes of the disease. The denial system is confronted. An understanding of the nature and process of addictive disease helps to reduce shame and fear and increase self-worth. Through working the programme of recovery based upon the principles of the Anonymous Fellowships, there is gradual recovery of physical, intellectual, emotional and finally spiritual well-being. In time, the recovering person, by actively working the twelve suggested steps of the recovery programme on a continuing daily basis, becomes progressively more secure in his or her recovery. Dealing with guilt for past behaviour by making direct amends to those who have been harmed, dealing with shame by accepting one's self as having an illness and therefore worthy of self-forgiveness, and dealing with damaged relationships by being honest, open-minded and willing, all help to re-establish the general sense of well-being that is the hallmark of someone in recovery.

But it is not easy. The programme is simple but certainly not easy and most of all it is individual: nobody can give recovery to anyone else, each recovering person has to work for his or her own recovery. Even a temporary relapse back to old behaviour and its damaging consequences may itself hopefully be a therapeutic process because it acts as a reminder that recovery is a continuing process that has to be worked for on a continuing basis by each and every recovering person.

The goals are worth the work. Not only is the destruction of addictive disease replaced by the creativity of recovery but the progressive return of spiritual values such as faith, hope, love, trust, honesty, forgiveness, empathy, gratitude and the return of child-like innocence in the appreciation of the beauty of the world, make recovery synonymous with the treasure of life itself.

The understanding of recovery as a process is still in its formative years. Not only is each person's recovery a highly individual process but also the ideas and techniques of individual recovery, group processes and treatment centre programmes are all continuingly and progressively evolving.

The stimulus of individual and group recovery and of working in the professional field of addictive disease and recovery is that each new discovery brings not only its own understanding and rewards but also the promise of more.

What follows in this Promis Handbook is simply the statement of where we think we are now. The important feature, however, is not the passing snap-shot but the journey itself. Understanding recovery is itself a progressive and unending process that brings immeasurable rewards to all who share "the road less travelled".

6. Recovery

What is recovery?

The capacity to sustain a potentially happy and fulfilled life without addictive recourse to mood-altering chemicals, foods or other substances and without addictive behaviours.

The alternative to the hopeless choice between continuing disorders of mood or continuing recourse to addictive substances or behaviours.

Consider the pattern of addictive disease:

the initial disorder in addictive disease is a disorder of the spirit affecting the sense of life, love, hope, trust and other senses.

this leads to a disorder of mood.

this is temporarily relieved by recourse to mood-altering addictive substances or behaviours. (fig x)

these bring problems of their own in their wake. (fig xi). These problems may further exacerbate the disorder of mood.

stopping the addictive substances or behaviours simply returns the sufferer to the starting position with increasing disorder of mood. (fig xii)

In recovery the Anonymous Fellowships, based upon the principles of Alcoholics Anonymous, provide successful continuing treatment for the spiritual disease that led to those disorders of mood so that further recourse to addictive substances or behaviours becomes un-necessary. (fig xiii)

How are eating disorders treated appropriately?

The acute starvation of anorexia may be life-threatening from malnutrition, disturbance of body fluid balance and decrease in defence against infections and should therefore be supervised in hospital or a specialist addiction unit. (This corresponds to the acute risks of

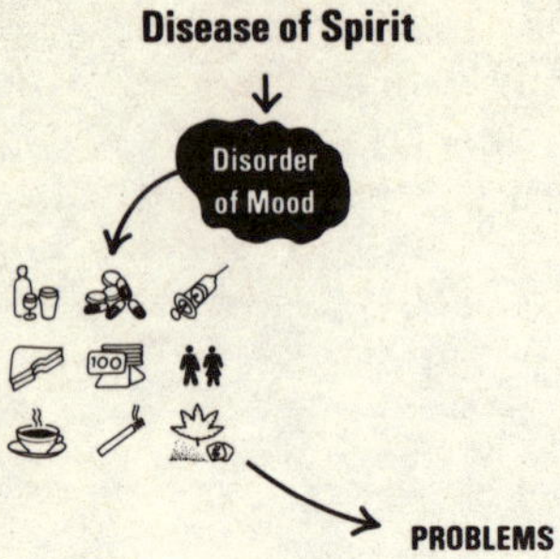

FIG (X)

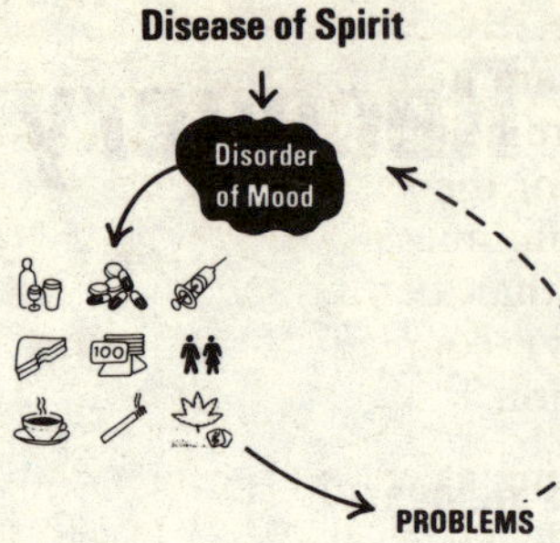

FIG (XI)

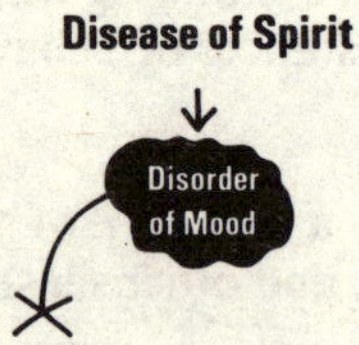

FIG (XII)

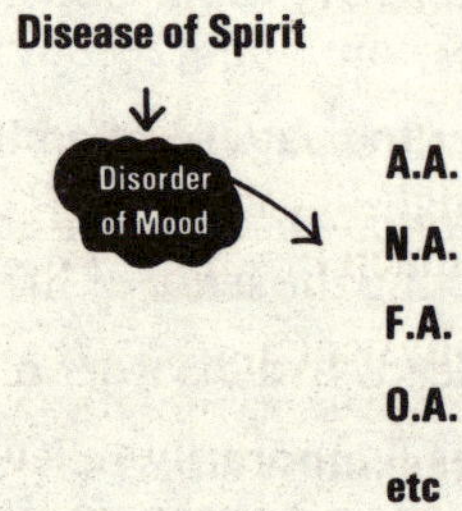

FIG (XIII)

epileptic fits or delirium tremens in withdrawal in alcoholism.) Beyond being life-saving there is no further place for hospital treatment of anorexia as it is primarily an illness of the human spirit and the hospital is important only for the treatment of acute physical consequences. Psychiatric hospital units for the treatment of anorexia commonly find that weight loss recurs after the patient is discharged from hospital.

Compulsive enforced vomiting may also cause acute disturbance of body fluid balance which may require treatment in a hospital or specialist addiction unit. The regurgitated acid from the stomach erodes the enamel of teeth and results in severe dental problems. As with anorexia, the condition tends to recur after traditional forms of hospital treatment in medical or psychiatric units.

Wiring together the jaws of compulsive overeaters; or performing surgical operations to reduce the abdominal apron or reduce the length of the intestines and hence reduce their capacity to absorb food; or inserting inflatable balloons through an endoscopic tube into the stomach; or performing liposuction to various parts of the body; all show no understanding of the primary spiritual nature of addictive disease. By concentrating upon the physical consequences, the surgeons are deluding themselves and their patients into believing that they are helping the problem and that they are providing encouragement for the future. In truth the exact opposite occurs - the compulsion continues as before and the physical problems return, sometimes worse than before and sometimes (particularly in the case of bowel surgery) coupled with medical complications from the previous operation.

Focussing attention on food is mistaken except in the requirement of the basic physical abstinence from sugar and white flour and specific binge foods and in acquiring the basic physical discipline of having three regular meals daily with nothing taken between meals. This physical abstinence is the equivalent of the Chemically Dependent patient needing to abstain from all mood-altering chemicals including those medicinally prescribed or obtainable in pharmacies or supermarkets.

Taking three regular meals with nothing in between removes the risk of "grazing" like cattle all day long and begins to re-educate the eye and the stomach in what constitutes a "normal" portion of food.

Basic physical abstinence can be exceedingly difficult. Residential care may be necessary not simply for the medical emergencies of starvation in anorexia or electrolyte imbalance in both anorecia and bulimia but also to monitor adherence to these requirements of basic physical abstinence. In some addiction units this monitoring is extended to patients initially being on "locked bathroom" status so that they may not use baths, basins or showers except under staff supervision, nor may they flush lavatories until after staff inspection. This supervision may appear somewhat unpleasant but the policy of these units is to break into the compulsive dependence upon enforced vomiting in the same way as the physical detoxification process breaks into alcohol or drug dependence.

In anorexia the first essential is for life-saving medical supervision. However, this nutritional "recovery" is only tidying up the physical consequence of the disease. True recovery begins with physical abstinence:

i. abstaining from sugar, white flour and specific "anorexic" foods such as salty substances and raw vegetables or "binge" foods that the sufferer knows may trigger a binge. In time, after strictly avoiding sugar and white flour, the number of other "binge" foods may be found to be reduced to zero.

ii. having three regular eals daily with nothing in between.

iii. ensuring that those meals each comprise a balanced adequate nutritional meal.

iv. avoiding artificial sweeteners.

v. avoiding self-induced vomiting, or purgation with emetics or laxatives or enemas, or the use of diuretics for "fluid reduction".

vi. avoiding excessive exercise.

and behavioural abstinence:

i. avoiding weighing more frequently than once a month.

ii. avoiding obsessing with appearance in the mirror.

iii. avoiding chunky clothing that disguises the true shape of the body.

iv. avoiding working with food in its preparation or serving.

v. refusing the help of family members and others who prepare "special" meals but having the same meals at the same time and in the same place as everyone else.

vi. learning to express feelings rather than suppress them through addictive processes.

It is of course easier said than done for someone suffering from anorexia simply to follow this recovery plan. It is little if any easier for someone suffering from Chemical Dependency simply to stop using alcohol or drugs. In each case the denial and the sense of compulsion of the addiction are almost insuperable difficulties for the individual to attempt alone. It is for this reason that the Anonymous Fellowships are so successful because they bring specific understanding and hope from previous sufferers who are now in recovery. The longer-term recovering member is able to give the newcomer a sense of identification that someone really does understand the problem from the inside and also a sense of hope that recovery is possible. This identification and sense of hope are technically possible in the home situation or in hospital but there is a serious risk that family members or medical and nursing staff will, by their own concerned actions intended to help the sufferer to eat, actually thereby enable the addictive disease to continue: there are few things the disease likes more than getting other people (rather than the primary sufferer) to take responsibility. Consequently, treatment for anorexia, after the initial life-saving medical supervision, is best managed in a 12 Step treatment centre specialising in eating disorders.

In bulimia or compulsive over-eating the same physical and behavioural recommendations apply as for anorexia.

The need for medical supervision may be necessary for those sufferers who repeatedly enforce vomiting and thus disturb the fluid balance of their bodies. For others, recovery may be possible simply through the appropriate Anonymous Fellowship, with or without some specialist counselling and therapeutic group sessions, or through a 12 Step treatment centre.

A specialist 12 Step addiction unit based upon the principles of the Anonymous Fellowships will have knowledge of the compulsive nature of all eating disorders and will also have an awareness of how family members and other well-intentioned helpers may unwittingly enable the diseases to continue.

The basic spiritual treatment of eating disorders is through the appropriate Anonymous Fellowships for Anorexia, Bulimia and Compulsive Overeating. Learning to allow emotions to be felt and to be dealt with appropriately in human relationships may be helped by specialised counselling within a 12 Step treatment centre specialising in addictive disease.

What is the first step to recovery in Chemical Dependency?

Stopping the use of the addictive substance or behaviour and seeking the help of the appropriate Anonymous Fellowship, most commonly Alcoholics Anonymous or Narcotics Anonymous.

Little if any spiritual recovery is possible without physical and behavioural abstinence. For sufferers from Chemical Dependency this means stopping the use of all mood-altering chemicals and also means reconsidering all behaviour, relationships, special clothing, hairstyles or other paraphernalia that may be associated with an alcohol or drug oriented culture.

What is the first step to recovery in other addictions?

As for the Eating Disorder or Chemical Dependency, stopping the use of the addictive substance or behaviour and leaving behind all relationships and special associations with the substance or environment of the addiction.

For compulsive gamblers it is advisable to abstain from all activities that involve risk-taking, other than the necessary activities of normal life such as crossing the road. Any activitiy that causes the same physical and emotional feelings as the particular addictive behaviour would be best avoided. Gamblers Anonymous is often the only help that is needed, although many sufferers also have other addictions. The 12 Step treatment centres are therefore also capable of dealing with gambling problems alongside other addictions.

The obsessive compulsive neuroses such as obsessive washing and the various phobias will require medical assessment but may receive particular help from Emotions Anonymous, which also covers a whole range of other emotional disorders that may be significantly disturbing to the life of the sufferer and be beyond personal control. Problems with addictive relationships, compulsive exercise taking, workalholism, compulsive overspending, and similar behavioural addictions may also best be helped through Emotions Anonymous and possibly initially through a 12 Step treatment centre. In each case, after any necessary life saving medical supervision, the initial steps are:

i. abstain from the primary addictive behaviour.

ii. avoid the circumstances and contacts associated with that addiction.

iii. seek identification and hope for recovery from the appropriate Anonymous Fellowship.

iv. consider specialist counselling or residential care in a 12 Step treatment centre if this is appropriate.

Addiction to (rather than simple excessive use of) caffeine and nicotine can be considered along with other addictive drugs. The caffeine addict or compulsive cigarette smoker may initially find it difficult to identify with someone addicted to Valium or Heroin but the stigma of addictive disease is inappropriate and the commonality of all addictions is considerable. A 12 Step approach to treatment for addiction to these substances is as appropriate as for addiction to any other drug.

The Anonymous Fellowships generally correspond to individual groups of addictive disease. For example, Narcotics Anonymous is open to users of any drug who wish to stop using and Over-eaters Anonymous is open to sufferers from any eating disorder. More precise identification may be available in Cocaine Anonymous or in Bulimics Anonymous but the risk of these smaller Fellowships is that the meetings may become weaker through lack of numbers and relative inexperience of recovery. A further risk is that the smaller Fellowships become so "special and different" that they may lose the wider identification with all sufferers from addictive disease and they may therefore be less exposed to the common humility that is the essential basis for recovery. Cross-addiction ensures that the weaker Fellowships receive support from members who have experience of stronger Fellowships but it may nonetheless at times be more helpful for a newcomer to receive slightly less individual identification but gain the experience of a stronger Fellowship.

The Family equivalents to the more recently established Anonymous Fellowships may not yet exist in this country or may be very rare outside major cities even if, as in anorexia, the primary problem may be life-threatening. The family involvement may be as addictive in its own right as in the case of families in which there is addiction to drugs. For these families, attendance at Al-Anon or Families Anonymous may be the best identification available and is therefore appropriate.

It is not known whether addictive disease is one disease that has different drugs or behaviours of choice according to each individual sufferer or group of sufferers or whether these groups correspond to one or another of a range of addictive diseases. Consequently, it is not known whether the ideal recommendation to any sufferer from any addictive disease of any kind is that he or she should be abstinent from *all* potentially addictive substances and behaviours.

From evidence on cross-addiction it seems likely that addictive disease is one disease with many facets and that any sufferer from any addictive disease might benefit from following the recommendations for all addictions. However, a practical consequence of this approach might be that few people would be prepared to consider such a sweeping initial recommendation. Nonetheless, once in recovery, the opportunity remains for the recovering person to extend his or her range of physical abstinence and, by doing this, the relapse rate may in time come to be less than at present.

This does not mean that total abstinence from all potentially mood-altering substances and behaviours is necessary before one can even begin to experience any recovery. Nor does it mean that failure to achieve total abstinence from all potentially mood-altering substances and behaviours means that one cannot achieve a considerable measure of recovery. Nor again does this failure to achieve total abstinence mean that one is inevitably heading for relapse or that it is necessarily a significant factor in those who do relapse. But it does mean that cross-addiction is a factor that may possibly be of some influence in all of this and that it is a factor that may need to be taken into consideration in the long term in attempting to improve the over all quality of recovery.

Initially, therefore, it is necessary to concentrate on the primary substance or process of addiction because this may be life-threatening.

How long does it take to recover from Eating Disorders and other forms of addictive disease?

A lifetime, one day at a time. Projecting into the future, wondering what may or may not happen and being fearful of it, is a common danger in addictive disease. While still suffering, the negative feeling of fearful projection may result in craving for the addictive substance or behaviour. In recovery, fearful projection can lead to relapse. Similarly, the thought of having to do or not do something "for life" can be overwhelming. Therefore, people in early recovery are advised to take life one day – or, in moments of acute stress, one hour or even one minute – at a time.

The opposite of projection is to mull over the past with resentment and regret. This is equally destructive of the time and creative opportunity of each new day.

Nobody can say that he or she has "recovered" from addictive disease. There may be no further use of the substance or behaviour of addiction but recovery from the "spiritual" disease is a continuing daily process. Just as someone who has short sight, penicillin allergy or diabetes never recovers from these conditions but can nontheless do or not do various things that diminish their effects or progress, similarly, sufferers from addictive disease will always have addictive disease even though they may no longer use the substance or behaviour of addiction. They can nevertheless do or not do various things that diminish its effects or progress. They are therefore described on a continuing daily basis as "recovering".

What is the course of recovery?

Just as addictive illness progresses on an irregular wavy course and is not predictable (fig (xiv)), so also recovery progresses on an irregular wavy course and is not predictable (fig (xv)). Just as in the progress of the disease there are times when things appear to be (and may be) improving, correspondingly, in the normal course of recovery, there will still be times when things appear to be (and may be) getting worse. Furthermore, in each case the sufferers or recovering persons may be the last people to be aware of these changes in themselves.

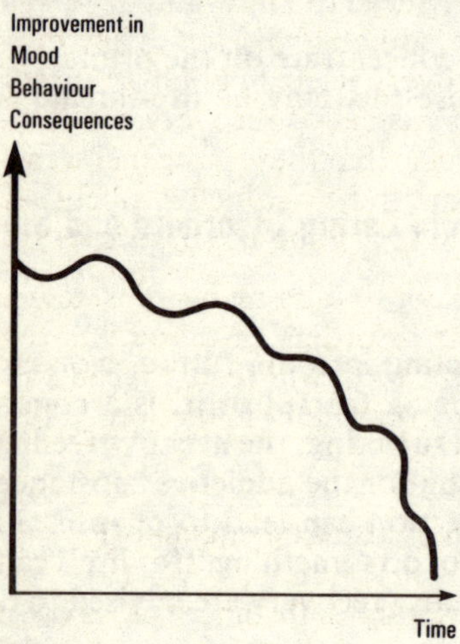

Disease
FIG (XIV)

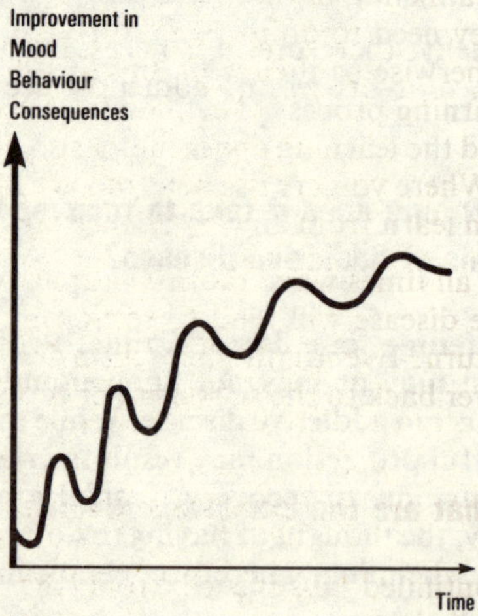

Recovery
FIG (XV)

Just as the disease varies in intensity from one sufferer to another so also the pattern of recovery will vary considerably from one recovering person to another. (See A,B,C in fig (xvi)).

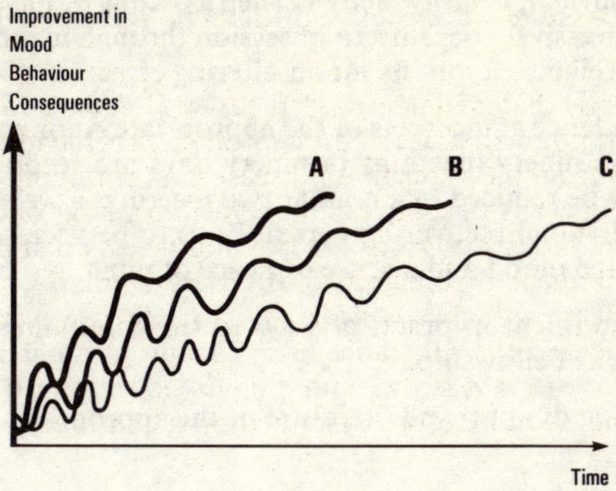

FIG (XVI)

Recovery gradually reverses all the characteristics of addictive disease. The previous consequences gradually resolve on their own as new constructive behaviour is substituted. It should be emphasised, however, that each person's recovery is idiosyncratic to him or her. Treatment Centres tend to find that they cannot predict which people are most likely to obtain lasting recovery. Some people who comply well with all that is suggested to them may have done little more than comply (incidentally, much of the "normal" first year of recovery is reckoned to be little more than compliance) and think erroneously after a few weeks of treatment that they have learnt all they need to know and have done all they need to do to remain free from addictive disease. They discover otherwise to their cost and this discovery itself may be an important learning process. The individual experiences of recovery are so varied and the learning opportunities so diverse that there is a general maxim, "Where you are is where you are meant to be", which implies that one can learn from any experience and put it to good use in recovery.

At all times when the need for active continuing recovery is neglected, the disease will tend to recur and the disorders of mood will tend to return. Eventually these disorders of mood will tend to lead the sufferer back to the substance or process of primary addiction.

What are the processes involved in continuing recovery?

Continued abstinence from the primary substance or process of addiction.

Continued avoidance of other substances or behaviours that may have a comparable, destructive, mood-altering effect on the individual sufferer. For people who have any form of addictive disease, care must be taken that a normal, healthy, activity such as eating or physical exercise does not progressively became an obsession through inappropriate use of, and later reliance upon, its mood-altering effect.

Regular attendance at meetings of the appropriate Anonymous Fellowship. Initially, ninety meetings in ninety days are recommended but later this may be reduced to a regular two meetings a week or however many the individual recovering person finds to be necessary to maintain a contented mood and a sense of peace of mind.

Regular commitment in practical ways to the continuing function of the Anonymous Fellowship.

Regular reading of approved literature of the appropriate Anonymous Fellowship.

Working the 12 Steps of Recovery of that Anonymous Fellowship.

Specifically working to gain insight into the characteristics of addictive disease and working to change one's understanding and behaviour in order to reverse them.

Maintaining Honesty, Open-mindedness and Willingness. The initial letters spell the word H-O-W and serve as a reminder of how recovery is achieved through all one's relationships.

Seeking the guidance of a sponsor – someone further into recovery in the same Fellowship and customarily of the same sex – to provide encouragement, challenge and guidance on the journey towards recovery.

Applying the principles of the 12 Steps in all aspects of life so that they become a natural way of life and provide the capacity to live happily and confidently without the need for mood-altering substances or behaviours.

The recovery process has been summarised: 'Don't use, read the book, work the steps, get a sponsor, go to meetings'', thus emphasising the simplicity of the programme that is freely available to all.

At meetings of the Anonymous Fellowships, continued recovery is sustained by sharing one's own experience, strength and hope and hearing others share how life was, what happened and how life is now. This process not only gives identification and hope for the newcomer, it also reminds the old-timers that they forget at their peril how life used to be. The disease appears to have a natural and selective ''forgetting'' mechanism, as is also the case in any major physical or emotional trauma. This may lead the recovering person to remember the mood-altering effect of the addictive substance or behaviour but selectively forget the negative consequences.

If people in recovery do forget that they have a lifelong disease and come to believe that they are "cured", then the original disease reasserts itself once more, not simply very rapidly down to where it was before but, in most common experience, worse than it has ever been.

The real secret of the Anonymous Fellowships is the paradox that one receives only what one gives. It is by helping newcomers, becoming a sponsor and by doing practical service of one kind or another for the group or for the Anonymous Fellowship as a whole that one gains greater insights into one's own disease and greater humility and security in one's own recovery.

In the long-term it is one's capacity to make open and honest relationships, outside the Fellowships as well as within, that makes the real difference to the quality of life and recovery. The Fellowships have a primary end in themselves in providing the route to sustained abstinence from mood-altering substances and behaviours. However, in doing this they also provide the basic opportunity to make happier and more fulfilled wider relationships.

To use an analogy from short sight: people who wear glasses are relieved of the effects of their short sight for as long as they continue to wear them and for as long as they remember that there are still some things (such as seeing clearly underwater) that they cannot do even if they are wearing glasses. Furthermore, by wearing them, they do not become better people or become equipped with supra-normal powers. They simply become ready to take their place alongside others, being neither special nor different, but at least no longer significantly handicapped.

Correspondingly, the Anonymous Fellowships enable recovering people to surmount their handicap for as long as they continue to follow the recommendations of the Fellowships and not believe that they are "cured" for all time and can handle "responsibly" the substance or process of addiction once more. People recovering from addictive disease are not special and different from other people (although they are fortunate in having a positive programme by which to live) but they are now able to take their place alongside others. They take their place in better shape than they themselves would have been without the privilege of working a 12 Step Programme.

Is there a risk that the Anonymous Fellowships can become a cult that takes over all life and leaves nothing else worth having?

Yes, the Anonymous Fellowships, like any other group for people sharing a common interest, could become a cult. The 12 Traditions of each Anonymous Fellowship are all derived from those of Alcoholics Anonymous and they protect against this particular risk by emphasising that the most important member is the newcomer and that leaders are but trusted servants; they do not govern.

In early recovery it is easy to develop the enthusiasm equivalent to that of some religious converts and this can be boring or oppressive to other people. However, the continuation of active addictive disease is even more boring and oppressive and the initial enthusiasm usually matures gradually within the first year of recovery.

It is understandable that the previous isolation of the disease results in a sense of amazement in early recovery on the discovery that other people have not only shared similar experiences but also similar thoughts and feelings. It is this sense of identification that gives hope to the newcomers that others will understand their fears and actions and show them the route to recovery. This acute sense of identification can be the alternative to a continuing sense of despair with a significant risk of suicide and therefore one can understand its importance in early recovery. Gradually, as recovery progresses, the sense of identification widens to include other members of the group and then others in the same Fellowship and then others in any Fellowship and finally anyone at all.

From the isolation of being "special and different", recovery is a gradual process of rejoining the human race. Although there will always be particular identification with others who share the particular form of addictive disease, the progress of recovery can be measured by the breadth of relationships: the wider the circle of friendships, and the greater the awareness of commonality with others, the stronger the recovery.

The 12 Step Programme becomes a positive addiction. Its purpose is not simply to help sufferers to leave behind their negative destructive addictions but also to help them to become enthusiastic about positive aspects of a healthy physical, emotional and spiritual life. The willingness to learn new things, practise new forms of behaviour and make new, constructive, relationships with one's family and friends are all part of the healthy re-channelling of time and energy that were formerly dissipated in addiction.

Working the 12 Step Programme is not an end in itself but the method by which the sufferer is transformed from negativity to positivity, from sickness to health and from a life of belligerence and blaming to a life that focusses upon creativity and an attitude of gratitude.

Can anyone recover from addictive disease through the Anonymous Fellowships?

Yes, anyone can, but not all do.

The "Big Book" of Alcoholics Anonymous describes some unfortunate people as being "naturally incapable of grasping and developing a manner of living which demands rigourous honesty" and says that "they are not at fault; they seem to have been born that way". For those who do not have addictive disease it seems incongruous that some sufferers will pursue their addiction to death, either through the consequences of the addiction or through suicide at the sense of hopelessness that is the hallmark of sufferers from the primary disease, – but that is the nature of addiction.

In the half century since the "Big Book" was written there has been continuing effort to reduce the number of people who fail to find recovery through the Anonymous Fellowships. Even today, the toll of addictive disease is still terrible yet many of those who die were aware of the 12 Steps and of the other recommendations of the Anonymous Fellowships. Whether they are "naturally incapable . . ." and "born that way" are the subjects of continuing study. It certainly seems probable that addictive disease has a genetic element although the strength of that genetic component may vary considerably from one individual to another just as the intensity of short sight or other conditions that are genetically linked may vary in different individuals. Whether "a manner of living which demands rigorous honesty" is all that is required is quite possibly true but there may be any number of blocks in the road towards that manner of living. It is the function of sponsors or professional counsellors to reveal and demonstrate these blocks and help to guide the newly recovering member to deal with them appropriately.

What are the common blocks in the way of recovery?

Isolation: The disease tells the sufferer that he or she is "special and different". The denial system tells the sufferer that he or she does not have the disease in the first place and that all secondary problems are really those of other people's distorted perception or a consequence of other people's actions rather than those of the sufferer. The disease

(Excerpts from p. 58 of "Alcoholics Anonymous" reprinted with permission of Alcoholics Anonymous World Services, Inc.)

leads the sufferer to believe that the world and other people have the problems and that he or she has the solution. The process of recovery involves reversing this belief.

Shame: The sense of hopelessness of the disease leads to a belief that the sufferer is not a worthwhile person. The process of recovery involves understanding the disease concept and accepting responsibility for future action to keep the disease in remission. This action involves making amends to self by coming to understand the power of the denial system that is the dominant feature of the disease. Thus, by increased understanding and by positive action, the sufferer is helped to accept his or her right to an appropriate place in the world, no more but also no less.

Guilt: In early recovery (and in moments of lucidity in the active disease) the sense of guilt can be overwhelming and devastating. Again, suicide is a major consequential risk. People with addictive disease may do terrible things to themselves and to others in the course of their illness. As the mind progressively clears in early recovery, the sense of guilt and remorse can be so powerful that the sufferer returns to the substance or process of addiction as the only known and practised method of suppressing unpleasant feelings. The process of recovery involves making an inventory of one's previous wrongs and defects of character, admitting them to one's self, to the God of one's understanding and to another human being and making amends to those one has harmed, except when to do so would injure them or others. This is the "rigorous honesty" to which the "Big Book" refers. The reason for the need for this rigorous honesty is that a continuing sense of guilt and remorse will reduce the sense of self-worth and well-being. This may result in further disturbance of mood and hence re-awaken the disease and increase the risk of return to the substance or process of addiction.

Grief: So much of life, its relationships and its creative opportunities are damaged or lost in the course of addictive disease that grief is universally a major factor in early recovery and also a major risk in the possibility of return to the substance or process of addiction. Further, there is a significant grief reaction to giving up the substance or process of addiction itself. This "trusted friend" (until it turned round on the sufferer: there is a Chinese saying "First man takes drink, then drink takes drink, then drink takes man") was the only known method of suppressing unpleasant feelings and, although maybe no longer trusted, is nonetheless sadly missed. In recovery the grief reaction takes two years to work through and the various components of grief have to be addressed and processed.

Anger: In many ways anger is the most powerful of the emotions to come to the surface in early recovery. There are feelings of anger and resentment at being singled out by the disease, at being unable to achieve the control one fought so hard to obtain, at being forced to accept defeat, at being forced towards recovery by the sheer weight of consequences and sometimes by the final threats of others who have at last truly come to the end of their patience and understanding, at having to give up the "trusted friend", at having to face up to issues one most wanted to forget and at having to make an inventory, admit one's wrongs and make amends. Each and every stage brings anger and with it the risk of relapse. In recovery, the anger has to be acknowledged and then dealt with constructively through working the 12 Steps. It is fundamentally important that these 12 Steps are actually worked rather than recited or merely thought to be nice in theory. Absolutely perfect adherence to the 12 Steps is unobtainable but each and every sufferer has the capacity to make progress from whatever his or her starting position may have been and this is all that is required.

Grandiosity: The disease tells the sufferers they are in control, they they are "special and different" and that all the problems are "out there", not "in here". The process of recovery is essentially one of reversing this process and of acquiring humility.

Is it necessary for family members to work an active programme of recovery?

Yes it is. Family members who are actively addicted to self-denial and caretaking for the primary sufferer have as much addictive disease in themselves as do primary sufferers.

Family members may suffer severe consequences from the active disease of the primary sufferer but similarly the primary sufferer may suffer severe consequences from the active "family disease" of the family member. A family member who is addicted to "fixing" others and being a caretaker for them can hinder the chances of primary sufferers finding progress or recovery for themselves.

The need to feel wanted by or necessary to others is in all of us but this need can be mangified to immense proportions in those who suffer from the "family disease". Expectations of gratitude and indebtedness may be submerged in a warped sense of "duty" or "normal behaviour". Sometimes these expectations of gratitude and indebtedness are the equivalent of taking hostages as if the family member is saying "I have done this for you and therefore you are under an obligation to do that for me". These obligations can be a heavy burden.

The family disease can be just as difficult to live with as the primary disease and can be a significant contribution to the relapse of the disease of primary sufferers in early recovery. "Self-denial" and "caretaking" have the opposite of the intended effect on the primary sufferer. They tend to aggravate rather than improve the poor self-esteem, poor individual coping skills and poor emotional maturity in the primary sufferer.

In the family disease "self-denial" and "caretaking" are the equivalent of an addictive drug, used as a mood-altering process regardless of the observable (but denied) effects upon self or others.

How do family members recover?

First by recognising exactly the same addictive processes in themselves as in any primary sufferer. "Self-denial" and "caretaking" are their particular "drugs" but the mental, emotional and behavioural aspects of the family disease are similar to those of any primary addictive disease. Sufferers from the family disease can no more control their addiction to "self-denial" and "caretaking" by themselves than any primary sufferer can control his or her use of the substance or behaviour of addiction in the absence of support from the Anonymous Fellowships.

Family members may have primary addictive disease of their own. (These people who have both the primary disease and the family disease are somewhat less than ingenuously referred to as "double winners".) In this case it is advisable to deal with the primary disease first, although frequently these sufferers only become aware of their primary disease as a result of exposure to the recovery programmes for family members.

They have comparable recovery programmes to those for primary addictions and the processes, needs, risks and potential blocks are identical. The capacity to achieve long-term recovery is also identical.

Attendance at meetings of the Family Fellowships, such as O-Anon, Al Anon or Families Anonymous, brings one among people who have had similar experiences and feelings and been equally confused, hurt, angry or depressed and taken similar actions out of confusion or despair. This is comforting and helpful in itself but, as with the primary Anonymous Fellowships, the real benefit comes from active involvement in working the recovery programme together.

Step 1 of the Family Fellowships is "Admitted that we were powerless over food (alcohol, drugs and other peoples' lives) – that *our* lives had become unmanageable". The emphasis in recovery is that the unmanageability of the family members' own life is a matter of personal choice: the actions of the primary sufferer do not inevitably dictate the reactions of the family member.

What is "Second Stage" Recovery?

The first year of recovery will vary from one person to another but for most people this first year in any Fellowship is spent mainly in compliance: doing what is suggested by people more experienced in the Anonymous Fellowships, attending meetings, contributing to them and giving practical service in them, progressively working the 12 Steps with the guidance of a sponsor and generally learning to use the various suggested techniques of staying away from one's primary addictive substance or behaviour and learning to deal with stressful situations in a more appropriate manner than previously. One of the most significant recommendations in early recovery is that close emotional ties should be avoided. Making a close relationship may lead to a false sense of self-sufficiency. Happiness may be misinterpreted as a "cure" of addictive disease - with disastrous results. Correspondingly, the break-up of such a relationship frequently causes such severe emotional pain that the old addictive substance or behaviour is sought in desperation for its mood-altering effect.

In the second year of recovery the recurrent cravings have mostly subsided and people in recovery develop progressively more insight into the nature of addictive disease in general and their own addictive disease in particular and also into the true, broader, meaning of recovery as something more than mere avoidance of previous addictive substances or behaviour.

Second stage recovery generally begins in the third year. In this the focus is upon improving the capacity to make open and honest relationships. Working the 12 Step programme becomes progressively more relevant on a daily basis in the recognition that it provides such a superb philosophy of life than many recovering people come to consider that they were fortunate to have addictive disease because it led them to the 12 Step Programme.

Also, in the second stage, people in recovery come to look increasingly at cross-addictions and at family issues of "co-dependence" in which the primary and the family disease feed off each other within a family or other close relationship. They also look at wider issues such as their own up-bringing which may have been in an addictive family and may have led to many grief or abuse or other issues that may still need to be processed with a sponsor or a professional counsellor if there is to be further progress in recovery. It may be unwise to attempt to tackle these various aspects of second stage recovery in any great depth before the completion of a full two years of recovery from primary or family disease because emotional and spiritual recovery may not yet be sufficiently secure to be able to take on these further challenges. It is for this same reason that training programmes in treatment centres are not normally considered for potential counsellor trainees until they have been in recovery for at least two years and preferably longer. A further reason is that it is commonly found that eighteen months into recovery is a particular period of disillusion and difficulty. As one would anticipate from the standard grief reaction commonly lasting two years, the recovery process is itself a grief reaction to the loss of a former "friend" in the addictive substance or behaviour. Through the help of this "friend" the sufferers dealt with the unpleasant feelings associated with the disappointments, disasters and challenges of life and now this "friend" has turned against them and the feelings have to be processed.

If one has significant cross-addictions, how many Anonymous Fellowships should one join?

Most people find that they have one primary substance or behaviour of addiction. Consequently, they are best advised at least for the first two years of recovery to concentrate primarily on just the one relevant Anonymous Fellowship.

In second stage recovery there is value in occasional attendance at meetings of other Fellowships if one has a measure of cross-addiction.

Some people have two or more equally strong primary addictions, for example anorexia and addiction to tranquillisers. In this case neither Anonymous Fellowship – Anorexics Anonymous or Narcotics Anonymous on its own would give sufficient identification and strength to be able to deal with both issues, – food and drugs. Therefore for these people it may be sensible to attend both Fellowships right from the start.

The Family illness is perhaps not a cross-addiction so much as an addictive relationship and a mirror-image of the various primary illnesses. While it is helpful for family members to gain a basic understanding of the illness of the primary sufferer, by going to occasional "open" meetings of a Fellowship for primary sufferers, so as to understand the disease concept and help to heal the blame and resentment that characterise active addictive family relationships, it is not helpful for family members to become regular attenders at the Fellowships for primary sufferers unless they themselves are "double winners" and have that primary addictive disease as well as the family disease. The prime need for family members is to attend the appropriate Family Fellowship and focus their attention upon their own recovery. Further, the experience of Treatment Centres is that primary sufferers have a far higher chance of sustained recovery if their family members are actively working their *own* programme of recovery in appropriate Family Fellowships.

It may seem extraordinary but family members may even feel more comfortable with active addictive disease in the home than with recovery. While there is active addictive disease the family member feels himself or herself to be "necessary" for fixing and caretaking and there is a clear family dynamic with the primary sufferer being the obvious "cause" of all family problems. When the primary sufferer is in recovery the family member, for all the protestations to the contrary, may be at a loose end with nobody to fix or control or take care of and there may be an uncomfortable awareness that the primary sufferer is not the only sick member of the household and not after all responsible for all its problems. This situation can be so threatening to family members that they may work against all the suggestions put to them and this may be a contributory factor in sabotaging the recovery of the primary sufferer, although it has to be said that the recovery of primary sufferers is always an individual responsibility.

Conjoint therapy sessions, where a counsellor (or preferably two) see both the primary sufferer and the family members at the same time, can be very helpful if well supervised but, if not, they can be very risky if they degenerate into a slanging match and leave behind more hurt than healing. The purpose of these family therapy sessions is to help each side to appreciate the pain of the other, caused partly by their own disease and partly by the reactions of the other side. Hopefully this insight draws the two sides together and helps to re-establish mutual understanding and trust.

Multiple conjoint therapy sessions where groups of primary sufferers meet with groups of family members can be helpful if the two groups are made up of strangers to each other. Where conjoint therapy is tried with multiple family groups (with the primary sufferers and family members coming from the same family) there may at times be little positive outcome because self-justification may take precedence over self-examination but, nonetheless, in skilled hands these groups can be highly constructive.

In second stage recovery, all recovery programmes are identical in their focus upon improving the capacity to make open and honest relationships but nonetheless it is still most appropriate to develop this understanding from within one's own original Fellowship and indeed to bring strength of understanding to that Fellowship.

Perhaps the most significant recommendation in all recovery programmes is that one should aim for progress, in particular spiritual progress, rather than perfection.

7. Relapse

What is relapse?

Relapse is the opposite of recovery. Recovery and relapse are both continuing processes and not absolute states.

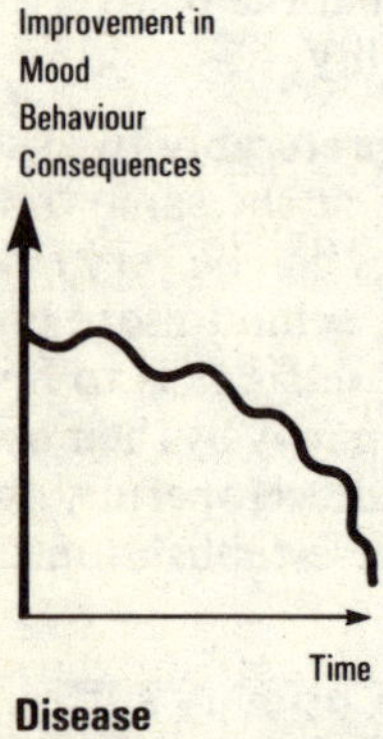

Disease
FIG (XVIII)

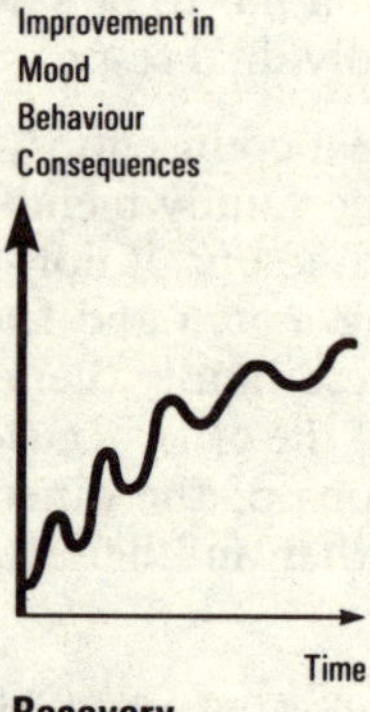

Recovery
FIG (XVIX)

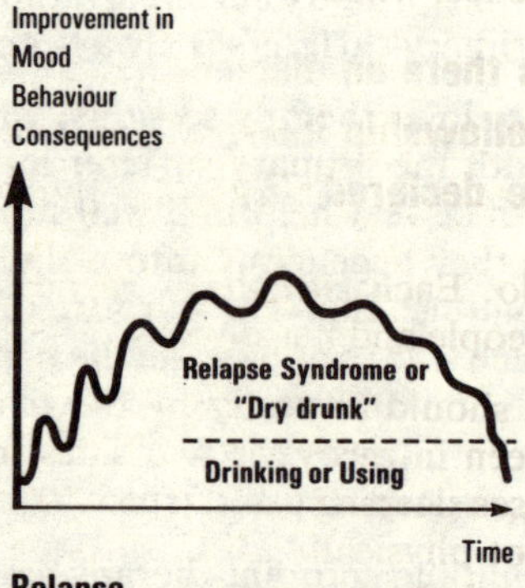

Relapse
FIG (XX)

Relapse can be seen in changes of mood before it leads back to use of the addictive substance or behaviour.

Neither recovery nor relapse is a straight line. Each follows a "wavy path". Just as the disease process has moments when things appear to be getting better even though in the long-term they are getting progressively worse, so also in relapse there will also be times when things appear to be getting better even though in the long-term they are getting progressively worse.

Relapse can occur at any time. The most characteristic feature of addictive disease is that it is a relapsing condition. It is never "cured": recovery is a continuing active process. If recovery is taken for granted, even after many years or even decades, the process switches over from recovery to relapse.

Seven

Relapse is the reappearance of the original illness. It is often triggered by an episode of acute stress and may be influenced by the failure earlier in recovery to resolve a significant issue. "Hanging on" to an issue rather than dealing with it through the appropriate steps - most commonly steps IV and V of the 12 Step programme - stores up trouble for a later day.

What are the signs of relapse?

Exactly the same as the mood disorders and behavioural characteristics of the primary disease.

The denial system is re-activated. The sufferer's disease gets back into "the driving seat" and he or she comes to believe that life can be managed alone and that it is questionable, despite all previous evidence, whether he or she truly has addictive disease after all.

Is there an element of "Catch 22" in this? - Agree with Fellowship ideas or risk being declared "In Denial"; relapse and be declared "Not to have followed Fellowship principles"?

No. Each situation - recovery or relapse - can be verified by other people and has directly observable practical consequences.

It should be remembered that one can not relapse unless one has first been in recovery. For example, a sufferer from alcoholism who still uses sleeping tablets, a sufferer from any of the eating disorders who is not physically abstinent from sugar and white flour, a sufferer from workaholism who exchanges work for physical exercise in similar quantities and a sufferer from the family disease who still searches incessantly for treatment or other solutions to the problems of the primary sufferer rather than accept his or her own powerlessness over the lives of other people and accept the need for personal recovery, are all still in the active phase of the disease even if they are regularly attending meetings of an appropriate Anonymous Fellowship. Their minds have never been sufficiently clear of the substance or process of addiction to be in any significant degree of recovery. When they get drunk, have a binge, take on yet another new project or make even more plans for someone else's recovery, they are not relapsing; they are still suffering, still believing that they can compromise with the concept of powerlessness over mood-altering substances and behaviours. They have not yet accepted the defeat that is the essential component of the first of the 12 Steps. This does not mean that they should not attend the Anonymous Fellowships. On the contrary, the only requirement for membership is a desire to stop the addiction. Further, it is only in the Fellowships that they will get sufficient identification with other sufferers to be able to see that there is hope for recovery when they do finally admit defeat.

Some people never do admit defeat. They never surrender but try to remain "in control" of their addiction. Some may die of the consequences of that addiction before ever getting into substantial recovery. Others may prefer to continue the addictive process rather than accept the need for personal change which they may perceive to be more painful than continuing the addiction. This is not a "Catch 22" situation of "heads I win, tails you lose": both the cause of death and the continuation of the addiction are observable independently by others outside the Anonymous Fellowships.

Comparing the previous experiences (prior to recovery) of those who recover and those who do not recover shows no significant difference. Recovery is therefore possible through the Anonymous Fellowships for anyone who wants it, regardless of how much has been lost or damaged, short of physical damage to the brain itself. Sufferers are never too young nor too old, too early in the disease nor too late to get into recovery when they truly want it: the "Big Book" of Alcoholics Anonymous and the equivalent "Big Books" of other Fellowships record many stories of recovery in sufferers who had been given up as hopeless. Today the Fellowships have many members who have made recoveries that can only be described as miraculous. There is nothing selective in their membership.

It has to be said, however, that some people continue their addiction to death even while making repeated attempts to follow the principles of the Anonymous Fellowships, yet still relapsing time and time again. Often they choose suicide rather than the continuing pain of recurrent relapse. To say that such people are "unfortunate", as does the "Big Book" of Alcoholics Anonymous (which is itself entitled "Alcoholics Anonymous") is true and indeed is an understatement. To go on to say that "they are naturally incapable of grasping and developing a manner of living which demands rigorous honesty" is also true but this may not be the whole truth. The preceding sentence, "They are not at fault; they seem to have been born that way" is itself an honest acceptance that addictive disease is stronger in some people than in others and that the acceptance of defeat and the wish "to go to any lengths" to get into recovery is ultimately a personal decision for each sufferer and not something that can be imposed by anyone else. Some people seem to find it impossible to make that personal decision. This is not a "catch 22": it is a statement of clinically observable experience.

The continuing work of the Anonymous Fellowships – and the definition of their prime purpose as stated in the 12 Traditions – is to carry

(Excerpts from p. 58 "Alcoholics Anonymous" reprinted with permission of Alcoholics Anonymous World Services, Inc.)

the message of recovery to those who still suffer. Specifically, this does not say that the message has to be received. Quite the contrary, it is acknowledged that carrying the message is all one can do.

There is no claim that the message will be received by everybody. It can be particularly difficult for family members to accept their own powerlessness in getting others to accept the message that they carry. As part of the denial of their own "family disease" they may believe that they themselves or the way in which they attempt to help others is what is inadequate rather than the capacity of the primary sufferer to receive the message of recovery.

The accusation of "Catch 22" is most commonly made by those who do not accept the disease concept and who may themselves be working professionally in the field of addictive disease, commonly believing in the psycho-social model of the cause of and treatment for addiction.

The challenge in return is to ask the accusers to demonstrate long-term recovery from use of their own concepts and methods of treatment. The belief that different treatment methods are needed for and tried on different populations of sufferers does not stand up to critical examination: the stories of those in recovery from addictive disease through the Anonymous Fellowships are so immensely varied that it is quite clear that this population has not been selected in any way. Even the accusation that the Anonymous Fellowships require a religious understanding and belief is unfounded. The "Big Book" of Alcoholics Anonymous specifically states "about half our original fellowship" were atheists or agnostics. Nor is religious conversion required: the God of the Anonymous Fellowships is as each member understands (or does not understand) a personal concept of God; the only unacceptable God is self. But in that there is common ground with Psychiatry: people who believe that they themselves are God are generally considered to be insane.

Step 2 of the Anonymous Fellowships states "Came to believe that a Power greater than ourselves could restore us to sanity". This implies the recognition that the self-centredness of addictive disease and the denial of its existance and of its consequences by the sufferer are insanity.

There is nothing self-congratulatory in accepting one's own insanity. The route to recovery is through humility. Again, there is nothing "catch 22" about this: it is observable clinically.

(Excerpt from p. 44 of "Alcoholic Anonymous" reprinted with permission of Alcholics Anonymous World Services, Inc.)

How can one detect the early signs of relapse?

First, by being aware that relapse is a process. The return to use of the substance or behaviour of addiction is only the final stage of relapse.

A "slip", a temporary recourse to the mood-altering substance or behaviour, may or may not lead on to a full-scale relapse. An accident may happen – such as when a sufferer from an Eating Disorder takes a sip of a drink that he or she was not aware contained sugar – and this would not even be termed a slip. However, if he or she, after the initial surprise of the taste and the recognised "feel" of sugar, took another sip "just to make sure", this would constitute a deliberate act and would therefore be counted as a slip. This needs serious appraisal because it may indicate that recovery is far more fragile than might have been appreciated.

The early phases of relapse in Alcoholism are known as "The Relapse Syndrome" or "The Dry-Drunk Syndrome". Similar early phases in relapse exist for all the addictions, including the family disease. This illustrates the behavioural commonality of all addictive disease. For example, "Alcoholism" is not the drinking and its consequences but the disease and the disorder of mood that leads to it. When this disorder of mood returns again in the Dry Drunk Syndrome one sees the clear distinction between the disease of Alcoholism itself and the consequences that follow it, if and when the sufferer later returns to drinking. Thus, the difference between the effects of Alcoholism (the disease) and alcohol (the drug) can clearly be seen in the Dry Drunk Syndrome. Correspondingly, all other addictive diseases can be seen in their primary form in the Relapse Syndrome phase before the sufferer returns (if he or she does return) to the use of the substance or behaviour of addiction.

The so-called "success" rate of substitution therapy such as Antabuse for alcohol, Naltrexone for heroin and minor tranquillisers for almost anything whatever, is because the prescriber may not understand the concept of the Dry Drunk Syndrome or because of the fact that minor tranquillisers and many other psychotropic drugs are cross-addictive with all mood-altering chemicals. It is a strange form of "success" that disregards the mood of the sufferer but simply observes abstinence from a specific substance or behaviour.

The long term success of a "sensible drinking programme" or corresponding "sensible eating programme" can only occur in those who do not have addictive disease in the first place. Indeed, the Big Book of Alcoholics Anonymous advises the unsure newcomer to try a sensible drinking programme in order to assess whether he or she is alcoholic or not. If the individual can always predict what will happen after the first drink then he or she is probably not alcoholic and may have no need of a 12 Step recovery programme and therefore cannot be said to relapse if occasionally he or she gets drunk. Correspondingly, if the individual can always predict what will happen after the first use of sugar or white flour then he or she may well not have an Eating Disorder and cannot be said to relapse if he or she occasionally binges. He or she may have emotional problems that result in occasional recourse to deliberate binges but that is not necessarily alcoholism or an Eating Disorder. By contrast, addictive disease is seen particularly when the alcoholic or eating binge occurs unintentionally or even when there was every intention of avoiding it.

Such "success" as there may be from legal prohibition of alcohol or other addictive substances, or simply through rigid "exclusion" diets, is gained at the expense of creating the suffering of "Dry Drunks".

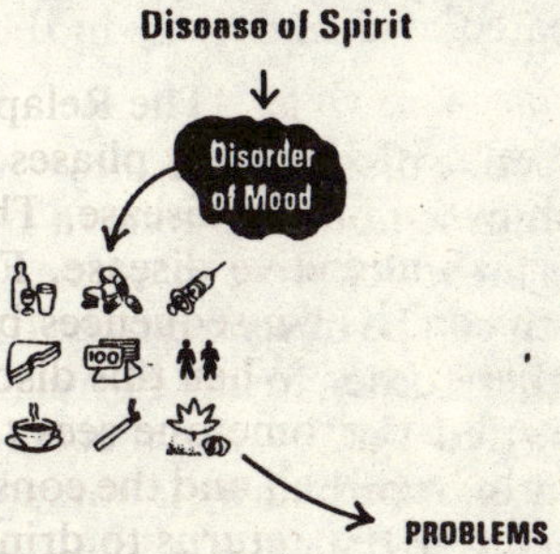

Addiction
FIG (XX)

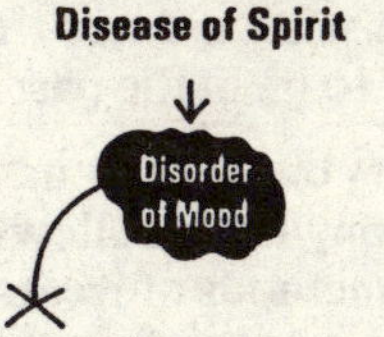

The Relapse Syndrome
FIG (XXI)

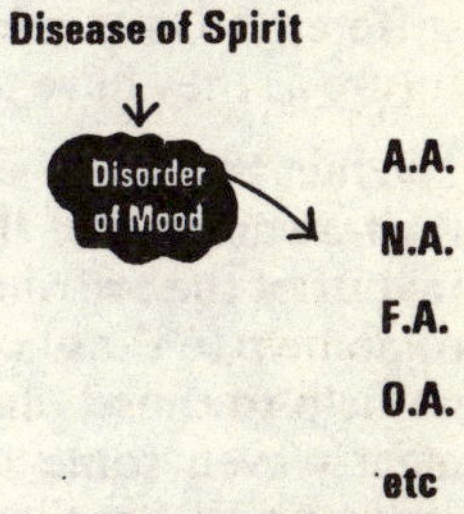

Recovery
FIG (XXII)

As emphasised, sufferers in relapse do not necessarily return to use of the substance or behaviour of addiction. This "non-using" state is *not* a "cure": it is simply a prolonged Dry Drunk. The "white-knuckle" sufferer who stays away from the substance or behaviour of addiction by grim determination, sometimes aided and abetted by non-addictive, anti-euphoriant or aversion-therapy drugs or processes is a pitiful sight. The spiritual riches of a full life are kept from the sufferer while the therapist colludes with the addictive disease itself. For example, giving Antabuse to a sufferer from Alcoholism, Methadone or Naltrexone to a sufferer from Heroin addiction, anti-depressants or tranquillisers to sufferers from eating disorders or to sufferers from the family disease or other addictions, or giving behaviour therapy or aversion therapy or electro-convulsive therapy to anyone suffering from addictive disease, is not only most probably inappropriate but cruel as well. Countless stories from the Anonymous Fellowships tell of barbaric (albeit well-meaning) treatment at the hands of the medical profession and other therapists.

The general lack of awareness in the medical profession of the nature of addictive disease and of the process of recovery through the Anonymous Fellowships is *scientifically* unacceptable. Surely, a clinical scientist should observe first, postulate second and treat third, not the other way round.

The fact that the Anonymous Fellowships are not run by the medical profession does not mean that they do not exist or that they do not work except for a handful of rather strange zealots. "Open" meetings of any of the Anonymous Fellowships are there for all to observe who wish to do so and it is a scientific and academic disgrace that experience of this successful method of treatment for a major disease is not a compulsory (or even an acknowledged) part of standard undergraduate or postgraduate medical curriculae. The experience of witnessing psycho-socially normal people from a wide range of abilities and backgrounds telling the stories of their individual experience and what has been done to them, would be the best method of ensuring that sufferers from addictive disease are not treated as dismissively in the future as they have tended to be in the past.

The fact that some sufferers die of their addictive disease regardless of their awareness of the Anonymous Fellowships is not an argument in favour of the use of other methods of treatment which were manifestly of no help to those who did recover and which can be observed to be of no help to those who still suffer. Some of these other forms of treatment - even some that are advised and carried out by the medical profession - are the clinical equivalent of the extraordinarily inhuman (and ineffective) previous "treatment" of cancer patients by pulling out all their teeth.

How can the recovering person protect himself or herself from relapse?

First by learning about the nature of addictive disease as a naturally relapsing condition and therefore being aware of the need for continual monitoring.

By getting a sponsor, one of whose functions may be to act as a mirror and reflect back the attitudes and behaviour of the sufferer, helping him or her to gain insight into self and establish goals for further improvement in recovery through guidance on the 12 Steps.

By listening, considering and making appropriate changes when others in the Fellowship give feedback. When family members, or other people close to the sufferer attempt to give feedback it may be resented and resisted by the reactivated denial system and lead to the opposite of the desired effect. Nonetheless, those who wish for lasting secure recovery will need to learn to consider feedback from any source and family members who truly desire long term recovery for their loved ones will need first to understand their own "family disease" and get into recovery from it before learning the techniques of giving open and honest non-judgemental feedback to others.

By becoming aware of one's own particular risks of cross-addiction and by avoiding substances and behaviours that are cross-addictive with those of one's own addictive disease. Being aware that feelings of negativity or excessive inappropriate activity of any kind can trigger the reactiviation of the disease process. Common risks are when the recovering person becomes hungry, angry, lonely or tired, the initial letters of which spell H-A-L-T.

By following simple recommendations consistently on a daily basis. Again, a healthy example is the instruction commonly given to sufferers from any form of addictive disease: "Don't use, read the book, work the Steps, get a sponsor, go to meetings".

By establishing pre-designed recovery protection mechanisms as a form of insurance policy, such as arrangements with trusted friends who will give open and honest feedback when asked - and sometimes when not asked - and help the sufferer to get to meetings and do whatever else may be constructive. Nonetheless, these friends will be aware that the sufferer ultimately has to make his or her own way back to recovery and that "helpful" actions should not serve to enable the sufferer to continue the recovery-threatening attitudes or behaviour without recognising his or her *own* responsibility for the consequences.

How does one intervene in relapse?

With great difficulty, particularly in the "Dry Drunk" phase before return to use of the addictive substance or behaviour.

Clearly, the earlier the better, but here the problem is that recovery itself follows a "wavy path" and one may rush in inappropriately and cause justifiable upset. One therefore needs to be sure of one's ground, exactly as for intervention in the primary disease, with documented evidence supported by others and expressed with humility and with care and understanding for the dignity of the sufferer.

8. Counselling and Treatment

What makes a good counsellor?

A thorough understanding of addictive disease and recovery, usually (but not exclusively) obtained by having the disease and recovery. Usually potential counsellors will need to be in recovery for at least two years before being considered for a training post.

Issues relating to the counsellor's own personal and family life will need to have been processed thoroughly because counselling other people has to be impartial (rather than be affected by issues in the counsellor's own personal life) and because the counsellor himself or herself may become unsettled when an issue being discussed with a sufferer may be too close for comfort to the counsellor's personal experience.

Usually counsellor trainees will be at least twenty five years old and, most commonly, older than that. Emotional maturation is arrested during the active phase of addictive disease and therefore the counsellor who is in recovery will need to have made up for this lost time for emotional development.

Intelligence is essential, although successful School or University examinations may not have been possible through damage to short-term memory (upon which facility most examinations are based) throughout the phase of active addiction. Whilst counselling is not essentially an intellectual process – mostly it depends upon a facility for empathy with a wide range of other human beings – it is nonetheless very demanding in the sheer volume of literature that has to be read and understood. Further, a dim counsellor is easily out-witted by the "cunning, baffling and powerful" addictive disease, as described in the "Big Book" of Alcoholics Anonymous, which is the basic recovery text from which those of all other Anonymous Fellowships are derived.

A natural aptitude for the work. This is not the same as being someone to whom other people often bring their problems; that does not guarantee the instinctive knowledge of whether something is real or merely a "try-on", or whether something that is being glossed over is really something that should be dug out and gone into in depth, or whether the time has come to say and do nothing other than give encouragement to the sufferer to work something out for himself or herself with the assistance of other sufferers in the group. All these facilities - and many more - correspond to the natural musicianship of the professional singer or the natural physical co-ordination of the professional athlete. One can learn the techniques of counselling just as one can learn to sing or to run but one will still be in a different league from those who were born with these skills. The paradox of counselling is that almost everyone in the caring professions believes that he or she is a "natural" counsellor when in fact very few have that natural skill. Frequently, the mistaken belief is that counselling involves telling people what to do in a nice friendly way and involves educating them with a few pertinent facts in a clear, easily memorable, style. In practice much more of counselling focuses upon perceptions and feelings rather than upon facts and the end result most commonly is helping the sufferer to focus upon a question rather than an answer. Confrontation of issues and attitudes will be polite and respectful in a professional manner but it may nontheless be a very painful process that would not in customary terms be considered friendly, although in truth it is a most fundamental act of friendship from one human being to another.

Emotional resilience - to feel one's own pain or tiredness or loneliness or what-have-you and be able to deal with it without "going to pieces" - is a fundamental requirement. "Burnout" is the spiritual condition, with severe physical, emotional, behavioural and practical consequences, that occurs when counsellors are unable to look after themselves appropriately. Sandwiched between the sufferers and the directors or managers of the institution in which they work (or overwhelmed by the pressures of survival if they work on their own) they may expect or be expected to carry and solve the burdens of both. Thus, institutions have a responsibility to care for those who give care through establishing mechanisms to evaluate and process the stresses of their work. The prime responsibility, however, rests with the individual counsellor to establish supportive relationships in which he or she is able to feel that stress is contained and processed and that feedback from those relationships is given in an honest and constructive manner. Burnout is commonly seen when counsellors have "family disease" of their own and are inappropriately self-denying and caretaking for their patients.

The fundamental requirement of all counselling is the capacity to observe one's own feelings, attitudes and behaviour by having open and honest interchange with others. This capacity - for emotional honesty and willingness to risk being hurt and acceptance of the need to make changes as a result of appropriate feedback - is rare.

The counsellor has to be at peace with himself or herself before being able to do work of any value with people in the active phase of primary addictive disease or family disease or, later, at any stage of their recovery.

Father Martin, an internationally renowned speaker and director of a treatment centre, summarises the requirements for counsellors in three C's: competence, charisma and commitment.

What are the prerequisites before counselling another human being?

Validation of the suffering individual, treating him or her with kindness, professional respect and dignity, being open and honest, separating the awareness of the disease from the understanding of the suffering human being, following the distorted reasoning and disturbed actions and accepting that they appeared to the sufferer to be most appropriate at the time they were committed.

Getting rid of "the bondage of self". The sufferer must know that he or she has the full attention of the counsellor and that the counsellor is on his or her "side". To be fully professional, one needs to express feelings and give responses to the feelings of the sufferer but nonetheless be aware that within that professional relationship it is not relevant that one should be personally liked or even appreciated. There is no place for aloofness and cold detachment in counselling but equally no place in the counsellor for a sense of personal need or rejection. Counselling is professional work, not merely a personal relationship.

Having no hidden agenda. The sufferer must know that what you say is the whole of what you believe and want to transmit. It is bad enough having the sufferer saying one thing but really meaning another without the counsellor getting caught up in the same macabre "game".

How does anyone intervene constructively in someone else's addiction?

First by recognising that one is dealing with an illness and not a moral issue.

By becoming aware that one's own denial system and that of the primary sufferer will tend to collude together to delay diagnosis despite obvious evidence of recurrent damaging consequences.

By recognising that one cannot "fix" someone else and that addictive disease has "Jekyll and Hyde" changes in mood and behaviour. Consequently one's own pleas and the sufferer's promises may all be well meant but nonetheless be all equally ineffective in controlling the longer term progression of addictive disease.

By not feeling personally hurt or professionally inadequate when matters get worse despite one's best efforts. That is sometimes the pattern of addictive disease.

By learning to let the sufferer take the full consequences of the use of addictive substances or behaviour. The short term risk is great but the long term risk of not following this course of action is even greater.

By accepting help in recognising one's own denial system and one's own contribution to dysfunctional relationships. In particular, one may need help to see that caretaking for other people, protecting them from damaging consequences and also doing everything one can to "help", may be having the exact opposite of the desired effect.

Sometimes a formal "Intervention" may cut short many years of further suffering. In a formal Intervention the people close to the sufferer - family members, a close friend, a close colleague, supervisor or employer, personnel staff or medical director - meet together to pool their information and rehearse their presentation to the sufferer. Group support gives the participants the courage to stick to their individual guns and know that they cannot all be misguided, regardless of the protestations of the sufferer when confronted even in an understanding and supportive manner. At the close of a formal Intervention when each member has said his or her piece, often in the manner "I care for you and I am concerned for you and therefore . . ." (avoiding the word "but"), the sufferer is presented with clear choices that have been discussed and agreed by the participants in advance. For example: "It is for you to choose between clinical or disciplinary action" and "It is for you to choose to seek professional help in the manner *we* recommend or alternatively terminate our relationship".

To present such stark choices on one's own, rather than in a formal Intervention, is commonly ineffective. The power of one mind and resolution pitted against one other is often insufficient and the simple passage of time usually weakens resolve and blurs the memory of precisely what was said or promised. The need for rehearsal of a formal Intervention is to strengthen the group resolve to give real positive help to the sufferer despite all the protestations, convolutions and deceptions that will be tried on by his or her disease.

In order to confront the denial system of the sufferer, but at the same time not cause it to be so aroused as to be counter-productive, it may be helpful to avoid specific terms such as "alcoholic", "drug addict", "alcoholism", "drug addiction", "anorexic", "anorexia" and substitute a phrase such as "stress and depression and problems with alcohol (or drugs or food etc)" or simply "problems in your life". In this way the primary sufferer – and the family members – may more readily accept the need for treatment even though they will subsequently learn that stress and depression are consequences rather than causes of addictive disease.

The timing of an Intervention is often most helpful at a moment when the primary sufferer is in a "circle of confusion". In this state he or she is putting out the mixed messages, "I need you to help me . . . get away from me". This most clearly illustrates the Jekyll and Hyde nature of the disease and this gives one particular insight into the concept of a disease of the human spirit parasitising the suffering individual.

As a general principle the earlier the better for an Intervention because less damage will have been caused by the disease and the denial system will be less entrenched. The disease does not go away if one ignores it: progressive decline is inexorable.

Perhaps the most important feature of an Intervention, in addition to giving an understanding of the distinction between the disease and the suffering individual, is to give a sense of confident hope for recovery.

What can doctors do to help intervene in Eating Disorders and other forms of addictive disease?

First acquire an understanding of addictive disease and recovery by attending six "open" meetings of Overeaters Anonymous, Alcoholics Anonymous or one of the other Anonymous Fellowships and two or more "open" meetings of O-Anon, Al Anon or Families Anonymous.

Observe that hypnotics, minor tranquillisers, pain killers and many other mood-altering drugs are cross-addictive with alcohol and with the various illegal addictive drugs. Extreme care should therefore be take in prescribing them at all: if the recipient has addictive disease, these drugs will make it worse.

Refuse in professional communications to use euphemisms or rationalisations: Eating Disorders, drunkeness or addiction should be termed as such and not covered up as "stress" or "depression". However, when dealing with the primary sufferer and attempting to get him or her to seek appropriate treatment through a 12 step programme it is best to avoid antagonising the denial system by being too direct. This would simply result in a battle of wills and the sufferer will always "win" that battle.

Do not provide spurious sickness certificates: these prolong the illness. If the sufferer loses his or her employment, this may be exactly the stimulus that ultimately leads him or her to seek recovery.

Use the help of members of the Anonymous Fellowships to help intervene in addiction in primary sufferers or in family members.

Recognise that the medical profession already sees the consequences of addictive disease in enormous quantity but frequently fails to perceive them as such. This professional "denial" can lead to the prolongation of suffering due to addictive disease in very many patients.

What can a Company do to formulate an Eating Disorders or an Alcohol and Drugs policy for the workplace?

Obtain the support of the most senior person in the Company and also of the Trades Unions.

Ensure that any policy applies equally throughout the entire Company from shop floor to Chairman of the board.

Obtain advice and support from local contacts in the Anonymous Fellowships, including the Family Fellowships.

Become aware of the experience of major corporations throughout the world who already have such a policy and who may have established Employee Assistance Programmes.

How does one intervene in the Family Disease?

In exactly the same way as for the primary disease. A group of friends, sometimes in conjunction with professionals, with an understanding of the family disease and familiar with the principles of the various Family Fellowships will confront the family member.

i. With understanding of his or her predicament.

ii. With observation that the primary sufferer has not been helped by the previous well-meaning actions of the family member while at the same time the life of the family member has definitely been harmed by various attempts to help or control the disease of the primary sufferer.

iii. With explanation of the disease concept of the primary disease and the family disease and with a clear message of hope for recovery and explanation on how to get help.

What does counselling in an individual or group context actually involve?

Imparting some factual information but more commonly referring the sufferer to resources from which he or she may find it for himself or herself.

Using a variety of communicative skills to transmit knowledge, understanding and feelings.

Being imaginative in presentation of ideas and practical exercises.

Being sensitive to non-verbal communication and aware of its significance.

Helping the sufferer to become actively involved in and responsible for his or her own recovery.

Helping the sufferer to see the pattern of previous illness and the principles of future recovery.

Confronting and challenging distortions of perception.

Probing, listening and reacting in a constructive, professional, non-judgemental manner.

Helping the sufferer to take the risks of self-disclosure and to acknowledge the need for emotional and practical support and help from others.

Helping the sufferer to recognise feelings that were previously suppressed by addictive substances or behaviours and to learn new methods for dealing with those feelings.

Helping the sufferer to develop an integrated sense of self.

Helping the sufferer to establish clear goals and to be oriented towards positive *action*, applying theory to practice.

Being aware of the nature of addictive disease and cross-addiction and its consequences and not frightened or shocked by it.

Being capable of crisis management.

Being clear-headed and aware of his or her own feelings, needs and resources, skills and deficiencies.

Having the insight and ability to share his or her own experiences, thoughts and feelings in a professional and personal manner that gives empathy and hope.

Being an example of spiritual growth and practical progress in recovery.

Remembering at all times how difficult is the demand and process of change.

Being capable of risking showing one's own personal vulnerability while still maintaining professional standards. Acknowledging the concept of the wounded helper being more effective than the strong.

Helping to facilitate group processes in an involved but non-directive manner, encouraging the group to take concerned responsibility for its *own* development and that of all its members.

Continually assessing the sufferer's knowledge, skills, blocks to recovery, attitudes and feelings and reflecting these back to the sufferer with the suggestion that he or she may wish to verify them with other members of the group. Even in one-to-one counselling the emphasis is placed upon group rather than individual awareness and support. No professional counsellor can "fix" or "caretake for" a sufferer any more than a family member or other concerned person can do so. Indeed, it would damage that person's recovery if he or she could be "fixed"; the recovery would be insecure and might be based upon the fragile integrity and perception of one counsellor.

The art of counselling is to do one's work professionally with respect for the dignity of the sufferer and then simply trust the process of the 12 Step programme and the effectiveness of the group, rather than try to manipulate, control or fix.

The essence of counselling in the "Minnesota model", used in treatment centres that follow the principles of the Anonymous Fellowships, is that each counsellor or other staff member is able to identify with a particular facet of an individual sufferer. Putting all the staff pictures together gives a more clear overall picture of that individual than any staff member could achieve alone. This collective picture is then reflected back to the sufferer with the recommendation that he or she finds out whether his or her contempories in treatment observe the same picture.

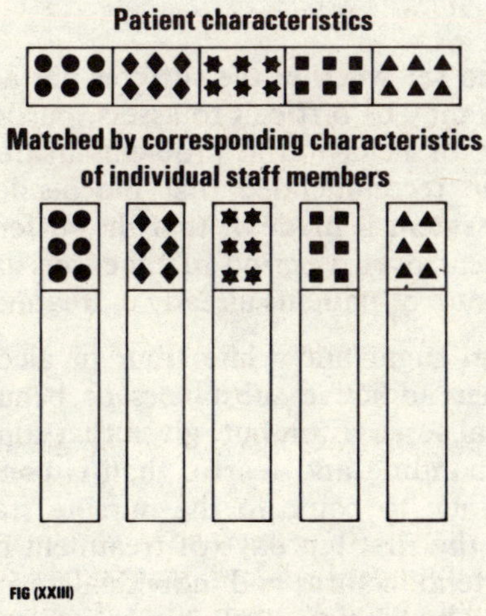

FIG (XXIII)

Thus, the essence of counselling in the Minnesota Method is not so much "I shall help you" but "our group see this in you, what does your group see?" The "healing" is therefore done between sufferers rather than from staff to patients and is the equivalent of the group insight and support that comes in the Anonymous Fellowships. The sufferers may not be able to see themselves but they can see each other and, by identifying features of themselves in the others, they gain insight into themselves and into their own disease. Equally, they also see the capacity for recovery in others and hence in themselves.

Specific issues may be processed in individual counselling. Grief, sexual abuse or other sexual problems and issues of sexuality, anger and resentment, shame and guilt and many individual blocks to recovery will need to be examined and discussed. "Processing" is the open and honest discussion of events and the feelings associated with them in counselling. It may – or may not – be appropriate to recommend the sufferer to refer these issues for group assessment. Sometimes "mini-groups" (which may be unsupervised by counselling staff) may be formed to discuss specific issues of common concern, such as issues particularly appropriate for women. Many women have difficulty becoming appropriately assertive, rather than submissive or domineering, in our male-oriented society and may find a mini-group of women helpful to examine this problem and process their reactions to it. Often, for these reasons, the sexes are segregated in Treatment Centres.

What is the customary programme in a "Minnesota model" treatment centre?

Initial assessment to see whether the sufferer has addictive disease at all. Sometimes this may be difficult to assess, particularly when there may be psychiatric or behavioural problems distinct from addictive disease. It may be recommended that independent psychiatric or psychological assessment is made or that the sufferer is admitted for prolonged assessment over a period of time (ten days or so) in daily contact with the group of patients already in treatment.

Detoxification from sugar and white flour or alcohol or drugs and weaning from other addictive substances or behaviours. This may require close clinical supervision but, given that supervision, is generally much less demanding and fearful than is commonly supposed. Patients will continue to come to the nursing station for periodic assessment during the first ten days of treatment but already by the second day they attend lectures and individual and group counselling sessions. Hopefully, by the time the lingering effects of physical addiction have worn off, there will be sufficient group cohesion and peer pressure to persuade the sufferer to stay in treatment and thereby counter-act the urge to believe that the problems were all a lot of fuss about nothing.

Technical assessments by medical, nursing, counselling, psychological and clergy members of staff giving a composite picture of the sufferer's clinical history and of his or her assets and deficiencies.

Throughout treatment there will be individual counselling and group sessions as well as lectures and other special processes such as relaxation therapy. Further attention will be upon general physical and nutritional health as well as on emotional and spiritual recovery.

Throughout treatment Reality Therapy is applied. The sufferer is confronted with truth rather than the version of it that corresponds to a false picture that only he or she perceives and finds acceptable.

The techniques of Rational Emotive Therapy are applied in which sufferers come to recognise that their thoughts (A) lead to feelings (B) which determine their actions (C) and that if they wish to change this progression they must learn to challenge the faulty reasoning in (A) and hence develop more appropriate feelings (B) and subsequent actions (C).

The fundamental belief of Dr William Glasser's Control Theory is similarly that feelings are the product of choice of perception. In clinical practice the sufferer is helped to see that there are other choices, other "pictures" that can be put into the mental library of how life is or could be, and that there is no need to attempt to control one's life by clinging to a fixed perception of reality that may have some validity for the sufferer but little validity for others. A light prism gives a practical example of how the same object viewed from different standpoints gives different images: one person may see only white light while others see all the colours of the rainbow, yet both perceptions are true to reality and not figments of distorted imagination. The sufferer from addictive disease, as his or her world progressively falls apart, may have clung desperately to some very individual interpretations of reality simply in order to survive.

The insanity of the disease – being compelled repeatedly to do things that are utterly self-destructive – requires constant readjustments to the "pictures" of reality. There is intense perceived pain in contemplating giving up the mood-altering substance or behaviour and making further major changes in these "pictures" of reality. By learning to go through the pain in a supportive environment, the sufferer learns to create new positive "pictures" and not to run away from emotional challenges by resorting to mood-altering substances or behaviour. He or she learns to listen to the other members of the group describe their "pictures" and this gives a wider perspective on reality than is possible for one individual in isolation. The sufferer's previous "pictures" tended to lead repeatedly to the same emotional responses to outside stimuli. New group "pictures" give him or her a new range of emotional responses.

Dr William Glasser's own model for addiction and recovery in alcoholism (outlined in the manuscript of a forthcoming book on alcoholism) is that the sufferer tries in vain to gain unconditional acceptance from other people. Dr Glasser identifies four primary needs (apart from survival through reproducing) in all human-beings:

i. power (competing; achieving; gaining importance).

ii. freedom (moving; choosing).

iii. fun (learning; playing).

iv. belonging (earning; co-operating).

Dr Glasser himself argues that unconditional acceptance is an illusion simply because we have to interact with other people who are just like ourselves and who share the same primary needs. Therefore there are inevitable limitations and conditions when we attempt to gain unconditional acceptance from other people. The false sensation of unconditional acceptance may come, however, when the sufferers from addictive disease are under the influence of alcohol so that the state of mind produced by mood-altering substances or behaviour is indistinguishable from the unconditional acceptance that they seek. This positive reinforcement of feelings in association with specific substances or behaviours becomes the basis for subsequent addiction. Dr Glasser believes that this specific susceptibility of the state of mind to mood-altering substances or behaviour in the sufferer from alcoholism may be genetically determined. Whilst other people recognise that the alcohol-induced sense of unconditional acceptance is a false sensation, the sufferers from addictive disease may cling to it even to death rather than face up to the reality of the need to accept any conditions in life. In recovery, however, they find unconditional acceptance in the concept of a Higher Power, and in the relationship with others in the Anonymous Fellowships and come to accept that real life in the world outside the Anonymous Fellowships inevitably imposes conditions.

Dr Glasser holds that alcoholism is a very real, concrete, disease rather than a disease of the human spirit or of the abstract senses but his understanding of alcoholism, based upon his practical experience as a general clinical psychiatrist, with no specific interest in the subject of alcoholism more than in any other, again fits closely with the expressed understanding in "Alcoholics Anonymous" and the experience of treatment centres using the Minnesota Method. As it says in the "Big Book" of Alcoholics Anonymous, "So our troubles, we think, are basically of our own making. They arise out of ourselves, and the alcoholic is an extreme example of self-will run riot, though he usually does not think so. Above everything, we alcoholics must be rid of this selfishness. We must or it kills us!"

Dr Glasser's Control Theory holds that people can be shown that they do have the choice of control over their thoughts and actions even though awareness of that choice may initially elude them. From exercising this choice they can influence their feelings and the physiological associations. Alcoholism is not the type of disease that is inevitably fatal: recovery is possible. Correspondingly, Alcoholics Anonymous emphasises that the choice of understanding and action involved in working the suggested twelve step programme of recovery will have definite beneficial emotional consequences as well as the obvious physiological improvements resulting from abstinence.

Help for problems in relationships comes from recognising that one needs to learn to go through the pain of disillusion that follows initial idealisation in order to reach the enlightenment of a mutually respectful lasting relationship, rather than following the repeated pattern of giving up and then renewing the search for a fresh "ideal"

The first two weeks of treatment focus upon the acceptance of Step 1 "We admitted we were powerless over food (alcohol drugs; gambling, emotions etc.) and that our lives had become unmanageable". Sometimes the mental and emotional fog is so thick and the denial system so intense that this Step 1 process takes significantly longer than two weeks. Needless to say, the sufferers in whom it takes longer tend to be those in whom the disease and its consequences are most intense and most obvious to everyone else. It should be remembered that recovery is a process of improving perception and is not merely an intellectual process: if sufferers could fully see and understand what they were doing to themselves, they would not have done it in the first place. The facts that they do fearful things to themselves and to others regardless of consequence and that they are unaware of the connection between cause and consequence are the essential psycho-pathological nature of addictive disease and denial.

During these first two weeks the sufferer makes an appraisal of his or her previous life and use of addictive substance or behaviour. This "life story" is written down by the sufferer and then read out to the group. There is no need at this stage to give explicit gory or shameful details but only to begin to recognise that the simple facts of the previous behaviour and consequences do not fit with the previous belief that all this could be managed satisfactorily alone and without outside help.

(Excerpt from p. 62 of "Alcoholics Anonymous" reprinted with permission of Alcoholics Anonymous World Services, Inc.)

(Adaptation of the Twelve Steps by Overeaters Anonymous reprinted with permission of Alcoholics Anonymous World Services, Inc. and Overeaters Anonymous)

The group reflect what they see of the sufferer's assets and defects (never defects alone) and he or she is helped towards the recognition that his or her previous life truly had become unmanageable and that he or she had tried desperately to control everything but was finally having to admit defeat and accept powerlessness. The advantage of telling the story to the group is that a group of sufferers from the same disease cannot easily be fooled, nor can they be harshly judgemental. You cannot pretend to people who, like you, have been pretending for as long as they can remember: they do not let you get away with it.

The essential process of Step 1 is surrender: the recognition that one is beaten, that one's own perceptions of reality are inappropriate and that one's life has become unmanageable and that one's own attempts to control one's emotions and use of addictive substances or behaviour have totally failed and always will fail. It is reckoned that Step 1 normally takes about one year to grasp and accept in its full significance. Treatment Centres take the sufferers through the first five steps of the recovery programme in as many weeks in order to lessen their dread in anticipation in the future and not because they believe that it is really possible to recover at that speed. The true pace of recovery in alcoholism is reckoned to be one month for every year of use. In drug addiction and in the eating disorders the process may be even slower because the drugs or the distorted eating pattern may cause more confusion and damage to thought processes and also because the sufferers may be young and may need to live through the emotional pain of adolescence that is necessary for maturity and which they earlier avoided by recourse to mood-altering substances or behaviour.

Each person will recover at his or her own pace, with the same individual variation as for any other illness, but generally the next week is spent on Step 2. "Came to believe that a Power greater than ourselves could restore us to sanity". To take away false self-reliance is constructive but even self-deception may be better than having nothing to put in its place. To expect a sudden conversion to spiritual belief is to expect too much (although it does sometimes happen) and fortunately it is completely unnecessary. The group itself is usually already perceived by this time as a source of comfort, strength, wisdom and support even though only a few weeks previously all its members were lost in active addictive disease. The group itself is commonly adopted as the "Higher Power" although some people may develop a more personalised individual concept of God or a Higher Power.

Subsequently, Step 3, "Made a decision to turn our will and our lives over to the care of God as we understood Him" is more demanding of one's resources of humility (as indeed are all the Steps) but it is really a logical progression from Steps 1 and 2. However, the capacity and temptation to take back this decision remain throughout the whole of recovery.

The strength of subsequent recovery will depend largely upon the willingness truly to hand over one's will and the outcome of one's life to a non-individual-human God. As Ernest Kurtz argues in "Not-God" (published by Hazelden), which gives the history of Alcoholics Anonymous, the process of recovery is essentially the recognition that one is not one's self in control of the Universe, nor even of much of one's own life, and that one is therefore Not God and nor are the mood-altering chemicals and behaviours that one previously "worshipped". One has responsibility for one's thoughts, feelings and actions but the outcome is in the hands of God. The self-centredness of addictive disease has to be changed to a life that is God- and other-people-centred if recovery is to have any lasting substance.

Step IV "Made a searching and fearless moral inventory of ourselves" is the first of the steps involved in "cleaning house" and in learning to see one's self as one really is – the good as well as the bad. This takes up much of the last week or more and is written out in precise detail. This is the time to make up for the imprecision of the life story in Step 1.

Step V "Admitted to God, to ourselves and to another human being the exact nature of our wrongs" involves a lengthy (usually several hours) session with another human-being (commonly a clergyman, specifically trained to be non-judgemental and non-denominational in the process, but sometimes a counsellor or some other person) to rid one's self of the continuing sole burden of shame and guilt. It is not the function of the listener to provide absolution, forgiveness or even "understanding" but merely to encourage the sufferer to admit to all the deeds that poison his or her memory and continuing poor self-image.

The process of making amends to others is in Step 9 and is not normally covered within a residential treatment centre but is left for later work with the support of the Anonymous Fellowship and guidance of a sponsor. It should be stressed that all the 12 Steps were established and practised long before the first residential treatment centre came into being and that many people today get better without the help of treatment centres or professional counsellors but simply by depending upon the Anonymous Fellowships. Furthermore, without the Anonymous Fellowships, the treatment centres and counsellors would achieve little or nothing. Sufferers get better in the Fellowships; treatment centres and counsellors are of value only in so far as they help sufferers towards an understanding of the principles and processes of the Fellowships. The value of treatment centres is in establishing safe, trusting and caring residential environments in which first exposure to the principles of the Anonymous Fellowships can take place.

The introduction to the first five steps of the Anonymous Fellowships while in a residential treatment centre is only an introduction. These same steps can be taken again with less apprehension and at a more studied pace under the guidance of a sponsor in the Anonymous Fellowships.

A few weeks of residential treatment are merely a scratch on the surface of the disease - but it is a deep scratch and it may help many more sufferers into recovery than might otherwise be successful through depending upon the Anonymous Fellowships alone. There are those who believe that hitting a *real* "rock bottom", losing absolutely everything and then struggling back solely with the aid of the Anonymous Fellowships, is the only true recovery. However, the "Big Book" of Alcoholics Anonymous, written a mere four years after the birth of that Fellowship, says "to be gravely affected, one does not necessarily have to drink a long time, nor take the quantities some of us have." In "Step One" of the "Twelve Steps and Twelve Traditions" of Alcoholics Anonymous it says "The first edition of the book 'Alcoholics Anonymous', published when our membership was small, dealt with low-bottom cases only. Many less desperate alcoholics tried AA, but did not succeed because they could not make the admission of hopelessness. It is a tremendous satisfaction to record that in the following years this changed. Alcoholics who still had their health, their families, their jobs, and even two cars in the garage, began to recognise their alcoholism. As this trend grew, they were joined by young people who were scarcely more than potential alcoholics. They were spared that last ten or fifteen years of literal hell the rest of us had gone through". Thus it is possible to hit a spiritual "rock bottom" in addictive disease while still having employment, family and possessions: each person's disease and recovery is unique to him or her. The same general principles apply to all forms of addictive disease and to recovery in any of the Anonymous Fellowships.

What happens after recovering people leave treatment?

Again it should be emphasised that many sufferers never receive counselling (except from a sponsor) or go into residential treatment in the first place and that residential treatment centres have no place other than to help sufferers remove blocks to their understanding of the principles of recovery of the Anonymous Fellowships. Thus, during treatment there are visits to some meetings of appropriate Anonymous Fellowships outside the treatment centre so that there is prepara-

(Excerpt from p. 33 of "Alcoholics Anonymous" reprinted with permission of Alcoholics Anonymous World Services, Inc.)

(Excerpt from p. 23 of "Twelve Steps and Twelve Traditions" reprinted with permission of Alcoholics Anonymous World Services, Inc.)

tion for long-term commitment to recovery through the Anonymous Fellowships.

Most sufferers are able to return to their own homes and employment after the completion of four or five weeks of residential treatment. Some sufferers, notably juveniles and, in particular, sufferers from anorexia, commonly take six to eight weeks because they have not been accustomed in their earlier lives to dealing with emotional pain except by recourse to mood-altering substances or processes. New skills and basic trust in new processes take time to acquire.

Quite frequently a sufferer in early recovery will "slip", having a temporary "experiment" with the substance or behaviour of addiction. This "field research" is commonplace and is simply the sufferer testing whether what he or she has learnt in treatment is really true in the outside world. The discovery that it is true can be a frightening and instructive process. "Slips" can occur at any time in recovery, even after many years or decades and can be much more distressing than the simple term implies. Often they result from particularly stressful circumstances but they may simply be a moment of carelessness. Repeated slips may mean that recovery was never clearly established in the first place or they may be an indication of the beginning of a full-scale relapse.

Some sufferers have such intense addictive disease or have sustained such significant emotional and other damage that they may require extended primary care lasting many weeks or months to gain gradual, gentle understanding of the disease process and of the beginnings of recovery.

Some sufferers, again particularly the juveniles but also those suffering severely from any of the Eating Disorders may require long-term (from a minimum of three months to more than a year) support in a half-way house. These establishments are sited in the community at large and are half-way between continuing treatment and a full return to the outside world. These sufferers in early recovery continue to live in a group, receiving some counselling and giving each other support and feedback and often going together to meetings of the Anonymous Fellowships. Often they will take up voluntary or paid employment during most of the day as part of gradual re-integration into society. The employment they take may have no connection with their previous skills or employment but serves as a temporary measure to raise self-esteem by doing something positive.

After-care sessions initially on a weekly basis but later less frequently, are recommended for up to two years. In these groups, particular difficulties are discussed with the group and with the counsellor. However, it is important that after-care does not become a substitute for attendance at meetings of the Anonymous Fellowships or for actually working the suggested 12 Steps of recovery or for establishing a continuing relationship with a sponsor. Recovery takes place in the Fellowships, after-care counselling is a bonus.

Do family members ever require residential treatment?

Yes, family members can have addictive disease that is life-threatening: their own "Family Disease" can drive them to distraction and despair (frequently misdiagnosed simply as a reactive depression) and they may even commit suicide.

Residential programmes for family members normally last five days, but may be significantly longer, and are separate from the recovery programmes for sufferers from the primary disease. Some conjoint therapy sessions between primary sufferers and family members are helpful to show each side the true feelings of the other, the need to accept and work upon one's *own* disease, and the need to separate in one's mind the disease from the suffering individual.

Vast numbers of sufferers from the "Family Disease" are given tranquillisers, anti-depressants and sleeping tablets and these can have a cumulative physiological addictive effect - and cause serious withdrawal problems even when there is no primary addictive disease. Further, these prescribed medications prevent emotional maturation through inhibiting the capacity to feel emotions and deal with them appropriately. As in the case of primary sufferers, these drugs tend to be significantly over-prescribed. Only in the case of sufferers from the "Family Disease" who genuinely have both psychiatric and addictive "Family Disease" are specific psychiatric drugs of any value and not in this case a definite hindrance to recovery.

Any family member of someone suffering from primary addictive disease may benefit from attendance at meetings of appropriate Anonymous Fellowships and may even benefit from residential care. The truth is that probably anyone at all can benefit from attendance at open meetings of any Anonymous Fellowship and from working a 12 Step programme. Anyone can benefit from the opportunity to work a programme that focuses upon honesty, open-mindedness and willingness and whose goal is the attainment of peace of mind.

It is commonly found that there is an interval of about six months between, firstly, the family member getting into recovery from his or her own "Family Disease" and learning to practise "tough love" and cease "enabling" the disease to continue by covering up its consequences and, secondly, the primary sufferer coming to seek recovery. Nonetheless, the purpose of the Family Fellowships is to help family members with their *own* feelings and recovery, regardless of whatever may happen to the primary sufferer.

What other help may be available in parallel to a 12 Step recovery programme?

Sometimes individual counselling may be helpful to observe and counter specific blocks to recovery. However, care should be taken not to use a professional counsellor as a "fixer" who enables the sufferer to avoid doing any real work of his or her own.

Behaviour therapy, Gestalt therapy, Art Therapy, Music Therapy, Transactional Analysis, Psychotherapy, Pschosynthesis, Psycho Drama and any number of other techniques may help some people who have problems with the process of moving rationally from thoughts to feelings and on to actions, even though these techniques have nothing to offer to the specific recovery process from addictive disease itself.

"Feelings Groups" in which a regular group of people in early recovery meet in a group, supervised by a professional counsellor, to discover and express their feelings in a safe environment and thereby gain awareness and practice for the awareness and expression of those feelings in the "real" world. Feelings that may have poisoned one's perceptions and coloured one's actions since childhood may be found inappropriate to be carried around continually in adult life.

9. Spirituality

What is spirituality?

A continuing sense of peace and hope and love.

Recognition that there is more to life than practical day-to-day matters: these are important but not totally important.

A sense of trust that one can learn from experience, however bitter and hurtful, and place it in perspective as a past event from which one can progress to create a richer, more fulfilling future.

A sense of commonality with other human beings.

An awareness that God, as each may understand Him, or a Higher Power of some kind (perhaps "the group" or "the creative human spirit within all people") can give one more understanding and tranquillity than one can gain for one's self in isolation and that this source of help is dependable.

Humility.

What has spirituality to do with addictive disease?

Everything: addiction is the devil, the spirit of evil, the destroyer. How strange and fearful a disease it is that tells the sufferer that he or she does not have it; that has almost incalcuable consequences and yet is so common that it becomes almost invisible by being thought to be part of normal behaviour until in its final stages; and that affects primary sufferers and family members alike in its terrible path of destruction. Addictive disease is indeed the devil.

Addictive disease primarily affects the human spirit. All its various manifestations are consequences of that affliction of the human spirit, either in itself or as a result of use of mood-altering substances or behaviour.

Addictive disease gets better with the spiritual programme of the Anonymous Fellowships and the various physical, emotional, mental, social and other consequences are able progressively to resolve, sometimes with outside help of one kind or another but commonly they resolve spontaneously.

How. does one achieve spirituality?

By working towards it gradually, one day at a time, as an integral and fundamental aspect of one's life with no remorse or regret for one's past and with no anxious or depressive projections for the future. The goal of spirituality is acceptance of one's self as one is and the corresponding acceptance of others. This does not mean that one simply forgets one's past. On the contrary, one learns from it. Nor does one forget the harm one may have done to self and others: Steps 8 and 9 see to that:

Step 8: "Made a list of all persons we had harmed, and became willing to make amends to them all."

Step 9: "Made direct amends to such people wherever possible except when to do so would injure them or others"

Further, the 12 Promises of the recovery programme in the "Big Book" of Alcoholics Anonymous, and which apply also to all those working the recovery programme of any Anonymous Fellowship, refer directly to really working Step 9:

"If we are painstaking about this phase of our development, we will be amazed before we are half way through. We are going to know a new freedom and a new happiness. We will not regret the past nor wish to shut the door on it. We will comprehend the word serenity and we will know peace. No matter how far down the scale we have gone, we will see how our experience can benefit others. That feeling of uselessness and self-pity will disappear. We will lose interest in selfish things and gain interest in our fellows. Self-seeking will slip away. Our whole attitude and outlook upon life will change. Fear of people and of economic insecurity will leave us. We will intuitively know how to handle situations which used to baffle us. We will suddenly realize that God is doing for us what we could not do for ourselves.
Are those extravagant promises? We think not. They are being fulfilled among us – sometimes quickly, sometimes slowly. They will always materialize if we work for them."

By working Step 6: "Were entirely ready to have God remove all these defects of character."

And Step 7: "Humbly asked Him to remove our shortcomings".

(Excerpt from p. 83 of "Alcoholics Anonymous" reprinted with permission of Alcoholics Anonymous World Services, Inc.)

These steps may tend to be overlooked or diminished in their significance but in practice they are fundamentally important. They involve trusting God or a Higher Power to be able to do things that are specifically practical: they are not simply a question of trusting to fate. They are the essential point of transition from fear to faith, from indifference to commitment and from self-centredness to God- and other-people-centredness. Those who have specific religious belief may find that the simple faith of childhood needs re-examination and perhaps re-forming in the mind and heart and not simply in a religious establishment.

Those who have been firm believers may need to ask themselves how it was that these beliefs and associated activities did nothing to protect them from the ravages of addictive disease. In this it is clear more than anywhere else that the Anonymous Fellowships are not religious organisations: religious adherence of itself from the days of Noah onward does nothing to help drunkenness nor Chemical Dependency nor even the behaviour of family members who cover up the problem:

Genesis IX v. 20–24 (translation: "The Way" Bible.)

"Noah became a farmer and planted a vineyard, and he made wine. One day as he was drunk and lay naked in his tent, Ham, the father of Canaan, saw his father's nakedness and went outside and told his two brothers. Then Shem and Japheth took a robe and held it over their shoulders and, walking backwards into the tent, let it fall across their father to cover his nakedness as they looked the other way."

Whatever it was that Noah was doing, it does not sound like social drinking and his sons' behaviour certainly qualifies them as family members.

Religious belief needs to be reassessed in order to provide relevance and commitment rather than mere lip-service. The process of truly handing over one's will and one's life in Step 3 and humbly asking God to remove one's shortcomings in Step 7 are no easier for the believer than for the non-believer in a religious God. In each case the important element is not whether one believes in a life hereafter but whether one believes in the possibility and actuality of God's influence and activity in the here and now and His practical care for each and every one of us. Recognising one's spiritual commonality with other people is a fundamental step along this path: no more is one "special and different".

We each have different skills in the manner of how we express our feelings but the capacity to feel is the same in each and every one of us. Some may deliberately repress various feelings but they are there nonetheless, as can be demonstrated in countless stories of recovery from addictive disease. For those who do not have specific religious belief, it may be helpful to consider this common element of human spirit in each one of us (call it "soul" if you like) as a Higher Power that is greater than self and which can be trusted to provide personal care. If one resolves to conduct all one's relationships on a "spiritual" plane of openness and honesty and appealing to the best within ourselves and each other, then this goodness and trust will be reflected from others - not always and not necessarily in the short term but the over-all effect in one's self and in one's relationships will be progress (rather than perfection which is unattainable) towards spirituality. Atheists and agnostics may in practice find this concept of a diffuse God or Higher Power residing in each one of us (and simply awaiting the eyes to see and the ears to hear) as easier to accept than do those with specific religious belief who may have much dogma and ritual to unlearn before they can grasp the concept of an ever-present God or Higher Power in each one of us, even though many religions specifically refer to this concept. Their problem may sometimes come from religious leaders who give the impression that God made the world as fit only for theologians to live in.

As time progresses in the Anonymous Fellowships, the strength of the urge to return to the use of the substance or behaviour of addiction gradually subsides, although it may pop up unexpectedly at any time. Consequently, commonly after about two years in recovery, the continuing work in each Fellowship, including these for family members, becomes identical. Focus upon self changes to focus upon relationships. Nonetheless, the starting point in the specific addiction of each individual is overlooked or forgotten at his or her peril. But, with that proviso, one person's attempts to make open and honest relationships with other people, and to be aware of the unit of spirituality (or soul) within each of them, are no different from the attempts of any other person recovering from any form of addictive disease.

Thus Step 10: "Continued to take personal inventory and when we were wrong promptly admitted it" unites all Anonymous Fellowships.

One common discovery in recovery is that it is often more difficult to receive love than to give it. For people whose addictive disease begins with a disordered sense of self, to love and appreciate one's self is hard enough and needs to be part of Step IV. Subsequently, learning to receive love from others and know that one is worthy (or unworthy) of it as one *is* - and not simply as a result of one's achievements - can be an enormous challenge. However, it is only as a result of learning to appreciate one's self that one learns that other people have the right to do so for themselves. Paradoxically, the most effective way of receiving love and learning to appreciate one's self is first to give it unconditionally to others. This recognition of the rights of others and the development of true appreciation of self is the essence of Step 10.

One specific technique that may be helpful in Step 10 is that of making a list of "affirmations". On this list one puts down those things one knows one is but tends to forget

e.g. "I am a worthwhile person, entitled to my life and to be loved as myself and not simply as a result of my achievements"

and also things that one would like to be:
e.g. "I am a good listener, considerate to the needs and feelings of others."

Daily statement of those affirmations comes in time to influence one's actions. The wish becomes reality when it is repeatedly put alongside the daily inventory of one's behaviour.

Step 11: "Sought through prayer and meditation to improve our conscious contact with God as we understood Him, praying only for knowledge of His will for us and the power to carry that out." Is the practical technique for achieving a sense of spirituality on a daily basis. Meditation is a worthwhile practical process for anyone whose head spins with day-to-day problems. The peace of mind that it brings gives a clear head to examine those problems, and put them into wider perspective, and to make plans to deal with them. But meditation is also worthwhile in its own right: it provides a quiet opportunity to become aware of one's own spirituality (or soul) and ponder the miracle of existence and even gradually come to terms with one's mortality.

We get so caught up with the hurly-burly of daily life and of the seeming total importance of the worlds of Politics, Law, Medicine, Commerce, Sociology and all the rest that we forget that, even in these days of staggering scientific advance, we still have no scientific answer whatever (except in physical evolutionary terms) to the three most fundamental questions of life: Who am I? Why am I here? Where do I come from and where am I going? Pondering these questions makes one realise that it is the so called "real" world that is the world of make-believe (despite it fundamental practical importance on a day-to-day basis) and it is the world of the abstract – of hope, love, honour, truth, beauty, trust and the rest – that is truly the world of reality. It is only when we inter-relate with each other that life has any meaning at all: the abstracts are our means of communication of spirituality.

Prayer presents corresponding difficulties to the problems of belief for people with or without specific religious belief. For the believer, prayer may have become an automatic process in which the individual is merely the utterer of prayers rather than someone truly personally involved in them. For the non-believer there are the questions of to Whom to pray and how and why and to what purpose. Believers and non-believers may each fall into the trap of self-centredness, hoping that a God of some kind or other will solve particular problems of the moment. But Step 11 specifically says "praying only for knowledge of His will for us and the power to carry that out". Thus, prayer and meditation are much the same process: being sufficiently calm to be able to become more spiritual, creative, loving and healing in one's relationship with one's self and others.

Prayer is seeking or asking and meditation is receiving or listening, each in an attitude of gratitude. This is not to say that prayer may not be directed towards specifics – but the answer may be "no". Each one of us, looking back on our lives will recall times when things went calamitously "wrong", despite all our fervent prayers of one kind or another that events would move in the opposite direction. Yet subsequently it may have turned out that we learnt a great deal from the "disaster" and the experience became of great value later in life. For some people this is evidence of God's "purpose". These same people may or may not have had specific "conversion" experiences and feel that they have been led to believe in a specific, personally caring, God. Others may have had no such experiences, and share no such specific beliefs, and yet still may recognise that much of life's experience is down to chance rather than planning. One can learn to reap benefit of some kind from any experience. The capacity to meet various turns of fate with acceptance and turn them to advantage is common to both believers and non-believers in a personal God. The need for strength to carry out specific tasks for which we may feel inadequately gifted or prepared is also common to both: the courage to launch out into the dark is the same whether or not one has specific religious belief.

Prayer is the process by which one recognises one's individual insignificance yet acknowledges one's capacity to tap into the strength and wisdom and love of God, as it may be expressed in specific religious belief or through the spirituality (or soul) of other people. In part, the strength one requires is to get one's own headstrong nature out of the way.

The "will of God" may be that which one finds in common with others in order to achieve the best, most creative, most healing and most loving individual development and mutual relationships. In this sense the Step 3 prayer in the "Big Book" of Alcoholics Anonymous can be said by anyone, irrespective of any or no religious belief.

"God, I offer myself to Thee – to build with me and to do with me as Thou wilt. Relieve me of the bondage of self, that I may better do Thy will. Take away my difficulties, that victory over them may bear witness to those I would help of Thy Power, Thy Love, and Thy Way of life. May I do Thy will always!"

(Excerpt from p. 63 of "Alcoholics Anonymous" reprinted with permission of Alcoholics Anonymous World Services, Inc.)

For prayer to have any meaning, the perception of God has to be individually relevant. For some people an orthodox religious God may suffice but for others it may be helpful for them to consider what they most value above all else in life and to recognise that this is most commonly a "gift" and not something that came about as a result of individual effort. It is a short step from considering that the gift comes from God to considering that it *is* God, as in the concept that God *is* love. Prayer may therefore be an expression of love and be no more complex than a reflexion on the various "slogans" of the Anonymous Fellowships, such as "Easy does it", "Keep it simple", "One day at a time", "Live and let live", "Think" and "Let go and let God". Each one of these, when put into practice, is an expression of love for self and others. To value them and to hope that one develops, as a gift, the calmness of spirit and strength of purpose to carry them out makes them into prayers. To move away progressively from the arrogance of self-will and towards humility is the purpose of all the 12 Steps. To learn specifically to ask for spiritual, emotional and practical help from other people and from the God of one's own understanding is the product of a thorough working of Step 11.

Finally, we came to Step 12 "Having had a spiritual awakening as the result of these steps, we tried to carry this message to compulsive overeaters and to practise these principles in all our affairs."

The spiritual awakening is not to be expected in a flash of light, although that can happen to some people in specific "conversion" experiences. More commonly it comes exactly as Step 12 says "as the *result* of these steps", all of which involve positive action.

Commonly in the Anonymous Fellowships there are two "dances". Firstly, the "Beginners Waltz" (1,2,3, - 1,2,3, - 1,2,3) in which the recovering person works the first three Steps but hesitates to make the personal inventory of Step 4. This Step clearly states that it is to be fearless and moral yet often it is assumed to be fearful and immoral. Sponsors guide the newcomer to put away these fears and simply note down how one is, the good along with the bad, the assets along with the deficiencies. The second "dance" is the "Fellowship Twostep" (1,12 - 1,12 - 1,12) in which the recovering person recognises his own need for the programme and immediately starts trying to get everyone else into it as well. "Twelfth Step Work", carrying the message to those who still suffer, can be most demanding and dispiriting and newcomers may have insufficient strength of spiritual reserves to be able to withstand the rejections that may follow. However, whilst it is true that the 12 Steps are in deliberate, careful, order it is also true (and emphasised in the "Big Book" of Alcoholics Anonymous) that one never achieves perfection. Consequently, in recovery, in addition to specific planned work on each Step, people repeatedly go backwards and forwards through all the Steps (particularly reminding themselves of Step 1) and including twelfth Step work, doing what can be done to introduce and welcome newcomers. Nonetheless, it is in twelfth Step work, as well as in daily acknowledgement of the need for personal recovery, that the Serenity Prayer is of particular value:

"God grand me the serenity
To accept the things I cannot change,
Courage to change the things I can
And the wisdom to know the difference".

Ultimately, the magic of recovery, first discovered by the founders of Alcoholics Anonymous more than fifty years ago, is that sufferers from addictive disease are powerless to help themselves but they are able to help each other and in the very act of helping another person find that they themselves receive help. Just as the newcomer "identifies" with the recovering member who is "twelfth-stepping" him or her by introducing him or her to the principles of the Anonyous Fellowships, so also the recovering member "identifies" with the newcomer. This twinning of human spirits gives substance to the recovery of both. The wounded helper helps and receives help. This is the function of the Anonymous Fellowships: they are "selfish" programmes in that recovering people focus upon their own need for recovery and are not thrown off course by the resistance or relapse of others. But the programmes are also truly "selfless" in that, through the 12 Steps and the 12 Traditions (which are the means by which the Fellowships service themselves), recovering people only keep what they give away: the opportunity and hope for recovery.

The relevance of all the 12 Steps is summed up in the second part of Step 12: "to practise these principles in all our affairs". The programme of recovery is not simply a method of combating eating disorders and other addictions. It is a way of life.

Appendix (i)

The Twelve Steps of Overeaters Anonymous

1. We admitted we were powerless over food – that our lives had become unmanageable.
2. Came to believe that a Power greater than ourselves could restore us to sanity.
3. Made a decision to turn our will and our lives over to the care of God as we understood Him.
4. Made a searching and fearless moral inventory of ourselves.
5. Admitted to God, to ourselves, and to another human beings the exact nature of our wrongs.
6. Were entirely ready to have God remove all these defects of character.
7. Humbly asked Him to remove our shortcomings.
8. Made a list of all persons we had harmed, and became willing to make amends to them all.
9. Made direct amends to such people wherever possible, except when to do so would injure them or others.
10. Continued to take personal inventory and when we were wrong promptly admitted it.
11. Sought through prayer and meditation to improve our conscious contact with God as we understood Him, praying only for knowledge of His will for us and the power to carry that out.
12. Having had a spiritual awakening as the result of these steps, we tried to carry this message to overeaters, and to practice these principles in all our affairs.

Note

i. Step 1 of O-Anon is:

"We admitted we were powerless over food – that our lives had become unmanageable.'

ii. Step 1 of Alcoholics Anonymous is:

"We admitted we were powerless over alcohol – that *our* lives had become unmanageable."

iii. Step 1 of Families Anonymous is:

"We admitted we were powerless over drugs and other peoples lives – that *our* lives had become unmanageable.

(Adaptation of the Twelve Steps by Overeaters Anonymous, O-Anon and Families Anonymous reprinted with permission of Alcoholics Anonymous World Services Inc, Overeaters Anonymous, O-Anon and Families Anonymous.)

Appendix (ii)

The Twelve Traditions of Overeaters Anonymous

One Our common welfare should come first; personal recovery depends upon OA Unity.

Two For our group purpose there is but one ultimate authority – a loving God as He may express Himself in our group conscience. Our leaders are but trusted servants; they do not govern.

Three The only requirement for OA membership is a desire to stop overeating.

Four Each group should be autonomous except in matters affecting other groups or OA as a whole.

Five Each group has but one primary purpose – to carry its message to the compulsive overeater who still suffers.

Six An OA group ought never endorse, finance or lend the OA name to any related facility or outside enterprise, lest problems of money, property and prestige divert us from our primary purpose.

Seven Every OA group ought to be fully self-supporting, declining outside contributions.

Eight Overeaters Anonymous should remain forever non-professional, but our service centres may employ special workers.

Nine OA as such, ought never be organized; but we may create service boards or committees directly responsible to those they serve.

Ten Overeaters Anonymous has no opinion on outside issues; hence the OA name ought never be drawn into public controversy.

Eleven Our public relations policy is based on attraction rather than promotion; we need always maintain personal anonymity at the level of press, radio and films.

Twelve Anonymity is the spiritual foundation of all our Traditions, ever reminding us to place principles before personalities.

(Adaptation of the Twelve Traditions by Overeaters Anonymous reprinted with permission of Alcoholics Anonymous World Services Inc and Overeaters Anonymous.)

Appendix (iii)

Suggestions for further reading.

"Alcoholics Anonymous" and "Twelve Steps and Twelve Traditions"
Alcoholics Anonymous World Services, Inc.

"Not-God" A History of Alcoholics Anonymous

Ernest Kurtz.
Published by Hazelden.

"Reality Therapy" and "Take effective control of your life"

William Glasser MD
Published by Harper and Row.

"The road less travelled"

M Scott Peck
Published by Century Paperbacks.

"I'll quit tomorrow"

Vernon E Johnson
Published by Johnson Institute Books.

"Stage II Recovery"

Ernie Larsen
Published by Harper and Row.

"Counselling for Relapse Prevention"

Terence T Gorski and Marlene Miller
Published by Herald House Independence Press

"The skilled helper".

Gerard Egan
Published by Brooks Cole.

"Facing Shame": Families in Recovery

Merle A Fossum and Marilyn J Mason
Published by Norton

"The best little girl in the world".

Steven Levenkron
Published by Warner Books.

"Excessive Appetite".

Tim Orford
Published by Wiley

"The Hidden Addiction and how to get free"

Janice Keller Phelps and Alan E Nourse
Published by Little Brown.